CW00376689

MORE SPAIN TOMORROW

Bob Able

CONTENTS

For Bee.

Without Bee, I could not be me.

With special thanks to **John Le-Sueur** for his inspiration, generosity and booze.

My thanks also to all the many readers who gave such encouragement and kind reviews to the original
'Spain Tomorrow'. Thank you all.

THE PARADE

The Spanish love a parade and, in Denia, despite being home to only some 44,000 souls, they really went all out.

At about 8:00 in the evening the Festes Major (of which more later) came to a close with the most elaborate, and long, procession of floats, led by a marching band.

The floats themselves, creating diverse tableau from a marauding dragon to Willy Wonka's Chocolate factory, covered a wide spectrum of themes; but all were sumptuously decorated and had obviously been the result of considerable effort.

How they were propelled was somewhat less elegant however, with a motley collection of elderly tractors, belching out fumes and an obviously 're-tired' lorry with the cab roof cut off and the dusty instruments and steering wheel revealed. Otherwise it was covered in plywood and polystyrene decorations and had a 'throne' for the fairy princess and her attendants who sat amongst the gaudily painted embellishments throwing 'confetti', which actually turned out to be the little paper circles you get out of office hole punches, into the crowd.

The lorry was the only self propelled float. The rest, and there were several, were obviously trailers pulled along behind the wheezing old tractors, which, by the look of them, had been working in the fields earlier in the day.

Some also towed generators to power the extensive lighting and sound systems, which blared away, seemingly heedlessly competing with the marching band.

The themes included 'Hollywood' with giant plastic 'Oscars' amongst the grinning and highly made up children and youths riding, who were dressed as everything from Darth Vader to Mr Darcy.

A clever but sombre float warned of the impending environmental crisis with plastic bottles and other detritus used to create ocean scenes and 'The Final Countdown' on repeat on the sound system.

At the other end of the scale, a sumptuously decorated float proclaimed the glories of some subterranean world where the participants enjoyed retina melting lighting and had wings.

Then there was the completely bonkers four

wheel bike (hired from the seaside tourist town on the other side of the mountain for the occasion, no doubt) with an enormous speaker strapped at a precarious angle to the front and ridden by four older youths, who had obviously been entering into the party spirit for some time. They veered madly all over the road in an effort to control the unbalanced and unwieldy contraption and it's yelling, laughing, vibrating and thumping payload.

And finally, bringing up the rear, along came the 'Willy Wonka' float which was easily the most professional, and must have been built for more than just this one event. It's glittering giant lollipops and rotating displays manned by children throwing boiled sweets to the crowds as the lights flashed and the generator towed behind revved up to keep pace with the demand for power.

But perhaps the craziest and most enchanting part of the procession was right in the middle, where the mother and baby group, all dressed identically, came along.
This unlikely group comprised tiny babies in arms (still dressed in the same outfits as their mums and older siblings) pushchairs, older children holding the hands of toddling brothers and sisters and, at their head, one smartly turned out little man, who could not have been more than 18 months old marching along determinedly, dummy in mouth and proud mum not far behind.

Just another reflection of this uninhibited fun loving country? Well, yes and no. This was actually, in part at least, a religious festival to bless the coming of age of the town's youth and celebrate their patron saint.

This procession was closing the event, after the paella cooking competition, where free food and wine were handed out, and before the fireworks; where free food and wine were to be handed out.

This marked the close of a two week festival which has been going on in this form since 1927. It seems the Spanish of all ages do not need any lessons in how to enjoy themselves, at all!

We were in for fun few weeks in Spain again!

Well, we would be if I could force the diagnosis to the back of my mind.

Ten days before we were due to fly to Spain, following some lengthy and not very pleasant tests, the diagnosis was confirmed. I had cancer.

We agreed with the medicos that a month in Spain would not make any difference so we grabbed a cheap flight and went for it.

Allow me introduce myself and the chief protagonists in our journey so far...

Bee, my wife of 30 plus years was, until she retired, a school cook; although to be fair she is also a qualified teacher who had worked in the same nursery school for many years in various roles, ending up as cook because nobody came forward to do the job and somebody had to feed the little darlings!

I retired early with back problems and a paltry pension and, if it was not for Bee's mother comprehensively messing up her finances, we would not have had the modest inheritance we were able to spend on buying our apartment in sunny Spain.

Milly, as I called my nutty mother-in-law, was a real character. Always in some scrape or other and, towards the end of her life was in something of a financial muddle.

If you read the first instalment of these memoirs 'Spain Tomorrow' you will know that she found she was running out of money, and when she finally admitted it to Bee and her three sisters, a rapid sale of her house had to be arranged and a one bedroom flat purchased to re-float her finances.

We will probably never know what she did with most of her money, but we did discover that Milly had taken investment advice from her window cleaner and had ordered solar panels from a 'cold-caller' after selling her house and exchanging contracts, just a few days before she was due to move out!

Against that background it should not have been a surprise that she needed to be admitted to a nursing home not long after her move, which in the frighteningly expensive commuter belt of leafy Surrey soon emptied the coffers further at an alarming rate.

Although she died some time later, her four daughters had resisted selling her flat to pay the nightmarish nursing care fees, and it was the sale of this modest property which generated our little inheritance and funded, more or less, the purchase of our property in Spain.

We love it, and Milly would have loved it too.

In her prime she loved travelling and was fortunate in that her late husband was a British Airways employee who got discounted or even free air travel. Unbelievably this amazing perk passed to Milly as his widow and she made full use of it. Those were the days when pensions and death in service benefits actually had some value!

Of course, as she got older, to the point where she had to give up her car, having crunched the front wheel and underside really badly, but claiming she had no recollection of how it happened, she became more sedentary.

On one occasion, before the house was sold, I stayed with her for a couple of nights when I had business in London and, as my best friend lived just around the corner, he and I arranged to meet up for drinks at the 'social club' at the end of the road.
This club is up a very steep hill from Milly's house but is a short, if taxing walk away.

On the Saturday morning in question, Milly asked me to get something from the end of the garden, explaining..
'It's all I can do to dodder to the bins and back these days, dear'.

Two hours later, when my friend and I walked into the club, there was Milly tucking into a huge full English all day breakfast with extra sausages.

'Hello, fancy you being here!' I exclaimed, while one of the group she was with chuckled and said that Milly walked to the club and tucked into a massive fry up every Saturday lunchtime.

13

So much for only being able to "dodder to the bins"!

Funny that the night before she pushed her plate away and complained that she had no appetite and could
"Only eat like a mouse these days".
Quite a large hungry mouse, it seemed!

But we should not be too harsh as not many years later she was finally diagnosed with "vascular dementia" which, as far as I understand it means that not enough blood gets to the brain.

Considering the active and fiercely independent life she had always led, which included extensive charity work, her decline was a shame and the world lost one of its true characters when she passed away.

Thanks to the unexpected inheritance however, our lives changed dramatically for the better so we owe her a debt of gratitude.

We had bought, modernised and enjoyed our apartment in Spain in 2016, at the time of the Brexit Referendum and the political pandemonium it caused.
In between fixing it up we had throughly enjoyed using it; albeit only in the school holidays when Bee was not working.
Now that Bee had retired however, assuming Brexit didn't stop us, we were determined to spend

longer periods of time there and enjoy the wonderful climate while exploring more of Spain.

The only fly in the ointment was my health scare which inevitably caused us some concern and made it difficult to plan trips while looming hospital appointments and procedures got in the way.

◆ ◆ ◆

"I'm selling it when you're gone," announced Bee.

We had been discussing how much time to spend each year in our lovely holiday home on the Costa Blanca, overlooking the Med again.

This, however, came as a blow. Didn't she like our well proportioned apartment overlooking the golf course, half way up a mountain, with two swimming pools and spectacular views to the sea any more?

"It's not that I don't like it, it's great; its just that I can't see myself coming here on my own.
So that means you can't die, OK?"

Obviously that was a relief. Well, sort of. It was quite relevant given the curved ball life had thrown at us recently and the issues I was struggling with.

But facing a lot more nasty and uncomfortable tests, treatments and operations when we got back, the hospital consultant had agreed that we could, and should take our planned break in Spain for a long 27 days in the sun.

Since Bee retired earlier in the year, we had been able to become the envy of our wage slave friends by taking such long breaks and, health allowing, we planned to continue to make them jealous. This was to be our third trip this year and was planned in October to coincide with the 'Ruta de Tapas' of which more later.

Now that we had a reliable car in Spain, currently stored in a warehouse by the airport, and given that, at least for the moment, everything seemed to work in our apartment, we were looking forward to using this time to see a bit more of the Country and take part in some local events.

Given also that the area is not tourist central, and that despite having many miles of fabulous beach on the doorstep, it is not overrun by ex-pats; this is a destination for the Spanish to go on holiday. As such the flavour of the events, the food and the language spoken are very much more Spanish than the plastic Disneyfied imitations available an hour and a half down the motorway in Benidorm.

Some people like their entertainment mass produced, and good luck to them, but we prefer to seek out what the more indigenous population traditionally enjoys.

Set in it's own little bay on a promontory not very near the main motorways or tourist routes, this area has, for now at least, kept it's identity and that we find most attractive.

The ex-pat population was probably still growing, at least until the Brexit referendum as far as the Brits are concerned, but wherever they are from the ex-pats only form a relatively modest proportion of the inhabitants overall. The numbers do however swell over the summer, when the Spanish descend on the area for their annual getaway.
The urbanisation our apartment forms part of is a short drive from the town and beach and overall is occupied by a mix of Spanish, French, German, Swiss, Dutch and even at least one Russian, who owns the Lamborghini parked next to our car in the underground garage; as well as several British.

We had bought the apartment with our unexpected inheritance, and intended to leave it to our two sons so that our grandchildren, should any appear, could holiday in the sun economically for years to come. Selling it was never a consideration and as we planned our next trip we knew we would enjoy ourselves.

BOB ABLE

COLD

I t was cold.

The first few days of October in darkest Norfolk had seen off the last of the summer warmth and on this night as I lay, unable to sleep, with the quilt pulled up around my ears, the coldness matched my mood.

I knew very little about what lay ahead, or the ins and outs of the medical terms; but to me, on this cold, cold morning cancer seemed to be like looking down a dank unlit tunnel from which there was no escape, with no re-assuring light at the end.

I suppose we all go through this moment, when you realise that you stand naked and very alone against this thing and that the only weapons you have are your own determination to fight down the rising panic and the love of those closest to you.

I got up and went to sit in front of the computer and I confess that, as the early morning light began to reveal a dry day, my personal raincloud produced a couple of drops which fell un-checked onto the silent keyboard.

But that was quite enough of this self indulgent and unproductive self pity, I decided, pulling myself together. There were plans to make.

We would be back in Spain in a few days and the world around us rolled on.

In the week that the always smiling Dina Asher-Smith and the stick thin but jolly Katrina Johnson-Thompson won gold medals in Doha in the athletic World Championships, Boris Johnson, our new marmite Prime Minister confused us all by telling a Scottish Court he would ask the EU for an extension to delay Brexit, but announced on social media that he would do no such thing.

The Brexit turmoil continued as, in post for just seven weeks, Boris had so far had to apologise to the Queen for lying to her, re-open the Parliament he had illegally shut, and had lost seven out of seven votes in the Houses of Parliament. As his latest plan for a deal with the EU was at first rejected and he was referred to as 'a chancer' by a very senior Lord in his own party, it was not a good start to his troubled spell in 10 Downing Street, and it did nothing to lift the mood in the Country.

In Spain the 'Gota Fria' storm had done untold damage to the more southern coastal areas but mercifully left our property pretty much untouched.

While his own swimming pool flooded and in between mopping up the torrential downpours at his own home on the mountain, our chum Peter Gunn was kind enough to take time out to visit our apartment and make sure there was no damage as we sat 3,000 miles away and awaited news.

Fortunately all was well and we could look forward to our next visit; and I couldn't wait to start the delightful 'Ruta de Tapas' (Tapas trail).

❖ ❖ ❖

June 2019

Our previous trip to Spain was in June and was very different in that it coincided with a massive heatwave across Europe which broke all sorts of records.
Our flight from the tiny airport in Norwich was on time for a change and we were surprised whilst waiting in the coffee bar which passed for the services at this little airport, to be hailed by an old friend.

Pam, compact and bustling, was a real Norfolk girl, and she and husband Arthur had delightful un-self conscious accents and generous natures.

'Blast me, Bob. Fancy seeing you hair!' She said. 'Are we now going on the same flight?'

I had first encountered Pam when she ran a Spanish Conversation Group which I joined in a mostly fruitless effort to learn the language. The get-togethers, which usually comprised gales of laughter interspersed with attempts to imitate the speech on an 'Easy Learning' Spanish CD, took place in Pam's dining room, and were made irresistible by the truly fabulous cakes she baked fresh for every meeting with the help of eggs from her handful of elderly pet hens.

Those half a dozen of us who attended were perhaps guilty of taking it less seriously than we might have done, but we all throughly enjoyed our weekly get-togethers which were made all the more delicious by Pam's warm character and generous hospitality.

As we caught up while waiting for the plane, and shook our heads in dismay that Flybe, the only airline flying to Alicante from Norwich, had decided to cancel the service from the next October, we discussed the news of the day concerning the effects of the heatwave, the dire warnings on the t.v. and what we might have to endure.
In darkest Norfolk, where the temperature rarely gets above 20 degrees, such an event was noteworthy indeed, but for fair skinned Pam with an apartment some miles south of Alicante without air conditioning, it was likely to be uncomfortable.
Being Pam she took it all in her stride and was looking forward to her trip.

When we got back she emailed me to ask how we got on and tell me that they had spent some of their holiday buying and having air conditioning fitted!

THE BULLS ARE COMING!

Our trip in June coincided with the 'Festes Major', and at the time I made these notes:-

Badger baiting, dog fighting, hare coursing and fox hunting. All obnoxious, all illegal and all, to a greater or lesser extent still going on.

In Spain (or even in the UK) few such events excite such outpourings of emotion - for or against - as bull fighting or bull running; yet this has been going on, according to Time Magazine since roughly 1591 in Pamplona and elsewhere, and continues energetically today.

In Denia the famous 'Bous a la Mar' event has been going on in its present form at least since 1927, more lately as 'entertainment' for youngsters coming of age and celebrating the 'Festes Major' in early July.

Before we go any further, let me say that the handful of protesters who lined the route of the bull run, wanting it banned, broadly got my support. But however you feel about it they were very much in the minority, judging by the huge crowds pressing for a better view and ignoring the claims that this was animal cruelty.

The adrenalin in the air was tangible and is the fuel on which events such as these thrive. As an outlet for this type of hormone, and no doubt given the money it brings to the town, the Authorities in Denia continue to support the event and actively encourage the youthful would be bull-runners by providing safety equipment, a large Police presence and ambulances on standby.

Although there is an expat population with perhaps different sensibilities about these things and emotions do run high, it must be said that because Denia is not simply a sanitised Spanish tourist town traditional values still hold sway here.

While the local press lauded or condemned the event, depending on their perception of the views of their readership (with the expat 'Javea Connect News' refusing to report on it at all, in protest), the event survives and prospers for now and, when during the heatwave and in need of liquid refreshment, we ventured into Denia and found the event in full flow, I scrawled the words below in my notebook about it:-

At last it is time for the 'Festes Major' in Denia, and we arrive in time for the first 'entry of the bulls and Bous a la Mar'.

There is a long queue for tickets to get into the makeshift three sided ring which, open to the sea on one side, would provide the focus of the spectacle. But, as there is no shade and we are enduring a heatwave, we decide against.

The streets, for a considerable distance, have been cordoned off with sloping slatted wooden barriers to contain the bulls as they run towards the sea, and provide an escape ladder of sorts for those foolish enough to attempt to run in front of them.

Whilst not on the scale of the famous Pamplona bull run, we have to view this event in context. This whole two week festival celebrates youth as well as the patron saint of the town, and is designed very much with those coming of age in mind.

As a result the town is full of young people in teams with tee shirts printed with the names of the members of their chosen group of friends, and out for good humoured fun.

The boys strut and pose on the road before the bulls are released and the girls, who seem to be in a competition to cut the absolute most off the legs of their jeans for the event, giggle and point from the safety of the barriers on which they sit.

After much shuffling for position, gossip and shouted greetings, the girls settle down and the boys, those who dare at least, mess about and look anxiously in the direction from which the bulls will be coming. They are watched over by a mixture of the local police and older men with responsibility for their safety.

The volume level rises steadily as the tension increases.

At last whistles blow and more experienced runners dash past to clear the way. The bulls have been released.

The girls, almost whinnying with a mixture of fear and excitement, move up the wooden defences a bit more as the boys, ashen faced now, but still offering macho comments to each other glance one last time to check their chosen escape routes are clear.

The bulls are coming!

A roar from the crowds in the distance at the start of the run

pinpoints their location.
The volume rises still further.

The older crowds behind the barriers push forward for a better view; and on the other side, the side the bulls will pass, the girls try to move their feet up just a tiny bit more in case.

The bulls are coming! The roar is getting closer!

Experienced runners and organisers start to move in the same direction as one.

The boys encourage each other and themselves with shouts.

The girls scream!

Here they come!

We can see them at last!

The boys start to dodge for position and their bravado evaporates as the beasts come around the bend.

The bulls are here!

Everyone on the road is running.
Everyone on the wooden barriers is screaming.

Everyone is sweaty, excited and, in an explosion of emotion, the tension is released.

The bulls are in a tight group of three or four, being goaded forward by a couple of handlers.

The boys jump and run and try to climb out of the way.

The girls scream and clutch at each other...

And then they are gone.

Just three or four little bullocks, none much higher than an adult's hip and trotting along at a pace dictated by their handlers, fast enough to provide entertainment, but not so fast that they might slip and fall or get out of control.

But the youngsters are still overexcited. This is what they have been waiting for.

The danger; the heroism; the tension; the cut off jeans starting to pinch, no doubt.

This is their day.

Their moment.

They have run with the bulls, and they absolutely loved it.

They would have some great tales to tell when they went back to school!

The latest news on the bull running locally appeared in the ex-pat focused English language 'Costa Blanca News' on 18th October 2019, when Samantha Kett wrote:-
"Whilst many towns across Spain are axing bull-running events and voting to remove them from local fiesta programmes, Pedreguer has gone the other way - for the first time the town hall plans to host the controversial act outside the July festival. As well as letting bulls and young cows loose in the streets, the events involve setting up bamboo fences of an eye watering 1.68m (5'6") and goading the animals into jumping them with crowds of onlookers entering the enclosure and waving sticks at them ...... Now Pedreguer - known by fans of these acts as the 'cathedral of bull-running' intends to

host similar events (from) Friday to Sunday inclusive, the first time it has done so in October."

Whatever we may think about it, and we will certainly not be going to watch, this spectacle does not show any sign of dying out soon, it seems.

PERFECT PEACE

We may not have one of the opulent sprawling villas, with infinity pools and tennis courts which dominate 'our' mountain, but we do share some pretty spectacular views with them.

Our apartment looks out to sea over the fairways of a golf course some distance below and we can watch the sun rise over the adjacent mountain nature reserve, and the sun set over the orange and avocado groves in the other direction.

We share two swimming pools (one of which is an elaborate affair with an island in the middle planted with exotic bushes and flowers) with just thirty or so other householders and enjoy the intensive work of busy gardeners who keep the grounds immaculate.

I regularly have to pinch myself to believe all this is really ours and, although the maintenance charges are not cheap, how lucky we are to have such a place.

We are surrounded by some really astonishing

properties, built into the mountainside for well heeled types from Spain and all over Europe and beyond. There are traditional Spanish style villas with arches and decorative balconies, sprawling ultra modern white Ibiza style mansions and just a few apartments like ours.

Kyero, the Spanish equivalent of the property search engine 'Rightmove' regularly advertises neighbouring properties at one, two or even three million euros and recently had a spectacular estate on the side of the mountain for sale, which we can see from our balcony, for a cool eight million euros!

Yet the view from our modest apartment is not substantially different from theirs.

Being in a greener part of the Costa Blanca, where admittedly there must be more rain than the arid, almost desert like areas further south, we enjoy delightfully mild winters and not quite such baking hot summers.

Up on the mountain there is always a cooling breeze in any event, so even on the most oppressively hot day we do not fry as much as those on the beaches five minutes away by car.

From our balcony as we look over the rooftops of the nearby town far below, we can see sailing and fishing boats flitting about and the hazy outline of an island, that the estate agent told us was Ibiza, on the horizon. It is rare, however, for us to see an aeroplane and we are never disturbed by traffic noise.

It may seem like paradise, and in many ways it is. Of course we would like one of the exotic villas our neighbours enjoy, and naturally we would love their money, but we can enjoy all the benefits of this lovely place despite our more modest means.

It must be said that some mornings here are absolutely perfect. When the sky is blue and the sea has no mist to spoil the view, the air is like crystal.

Spanish workers rise early to get some work done before the sun gets too hot. They are therefore lucky enough to experience this most beautiful time of day, and when we are able to enjoy it, it is certainly one of the best things about waking up in Spain.

We didn't need alarm clocks to get us up recently, however.

A little further up the mountain, amongst the stunning millionaires' villas, a digger trundled into position beside the road and the huge lorry which delivered it lumbered away.

The enormous contraption which remained was fitted with an aggressive looking 'jack-hammer' which it now swung towards the sheer solid rock face which rose from the road beneath one of the large villas.

We were not left wondering what was going on for long as, with only a reflective triangle on the road and a couple of ineffectual plastic barriers to warn oncoming vehicles of the obstruction, the mighty machine attacked the mountain with vigour.

The 'CRACK, CRACK, CRACK' of the hammer sent its resonance all over the mountain community, shattering the morning and removing all thoughts of a lie-in from all of our minds.

All day the brutal machine clacked and boomed away, and when we drove past on the way to visit the nearby town, we wondered if the villa directly above the hammering giant could survive the vibrations, or if it, like the lumps of solid rock being caused to fall, would collapse onto the road below.

Precisely what this monstrous contraption was doing was not at all clear until several days later when, after an almost continuous effort which must have driven those living adjacent to distraction, and with work often going on late into the evening, at last the results could be seen.

Our apartment is probably three quarters of a

mile from the scene of all this work by the winding mountain roadway, or half a mile as the crow flies. Those living in closer proximity must have felt every blow of the hammer and were no doubt doubly glad when it finally stopped.

The usual peace of the mountain morning, punctuated only by birdsong and the occasional distant shout of "Fore!" from the golf course far below at the bottom of the hill was resumed.

As we drove past on our way into the town again a few days later a large scar about thirty feet high could be seen in the steep rock, and a new vertical face had been created right underneath the foundations of the villa above.

Closer examination gave us a clue as to what was likely to be going on here.

A flat area had been created by the road with a little trench around the sides and a deeper excavation, about a metre square had been hewn out of the rock in the middle of the new sheer face at the back.

A thick electrical cable hung down from the precariously perched villa above and, after a little thought it dawned on us what was going to be built here.

'It's going to be a lift up to the villa, I bet,' Bee announced. 'And by the looks of things that hole by the road is to become a garage!'

No doubt she was right and maybe it would be finished by our next visit to Spain. But this must be one of the most costly garages ever built! Carved, as it was, out of the solid rock at no doubt great expense, to create a space for it before anything else could even be built.

The lift up to the villa, if that is what it was to be, might save the occupants a walk up a longish steep drive but it also gave us mere mortals an insight as to the affluent nature of its creators.
No wonder they call this 'millionaires mountain'!

ENCOUNTERS WITH WINE

I t is quite amazing who one meets by chance.

We had been aware that we had a new neighbour and had exchanged the occasional 'Hola' but, until we passed each other outside his front door, we had not had the opportunity to introduce ourselves.

Graham looked like a geography teacher, even down to the battered brown leather school bag he carried; but his work was much more interesting than that.
It transpired he was a wholesale wine merchant, with contracts to supply the local supermarkets and restaurants.

He also had a very talkative little black cat who handled the introductions for us!

It soon emerged that it was Graham's vast Mercedes parked next to our modest Ford Fiesta and that he owned property further along the coast but used his apartment close to ours as a base when in the area.

His little cat also regarded it as home apparently, and although much travelled, had her human provide a cat-flap with a sophisticated electronic tag lock to keep her visitors from gaining access to her private rooms.

We were more fortunate, however, when Graham invited us in and the conversation turned to his wine business.

'What sort of wines do you enjoy?' he asked, and as we struggled to describe coherently what we, as rank amateurs in this field preferred, he produced a portfolio from the school bag containing lists and tasting notes on all the wines he kept in his cellars.

Judging by the size of the portfolio, the cellars must be huge.

'Quite large,' he said 'It's a wide building on two floors and stretches from ... oh, let's see ... Well from about here to the swimming pool.'

The pool in question was about 80 metres away, so we were talking to the representative of a serious supplier here.

'It has to be large to keep our clients supplied, and it is pretty much rammed to the rafters most of the time.'

I enquired who they supplied.

'Well, a few of the supermarket chains and almost all the better restaurants locally, but its not all high end stuff, we cater to the lower end of the market too.'

To prove the point he produced a price list with really good wines we had heard of at prices about a third of what we, as retail customers, have to pay.

'As you see the mark-up on wines is where restaurants make a lot of their profit, but they don't like to offer the same stuff as the supermarkets or people might baulk at the prices.'

'I'm not surprised,' I said, 'Much more economical to drink at home, it seems!'

'Well that depends on what you like. The supermarket stuff can all be a bit similar and usually sells on price, but we supply a range of local Spanish wines that you are unlikely to see on their shelves which provide the restaurants with a point of difference. And some of the Spanish wines are really very good indeed these days.'

He showed us examples in the vast catalogue from both ends of the spectrum. There were wines we had indeed seen on the supermarket shelves (and bought) and wines which were only slightly more expensive but were, we learned, in a different league when it came to taste.

'I usually make up cases of various wines as samples for particular restaurateurs to try, so that they can decide what their customers like, and provide them with some guidance if they are not confident at tasting,' he said, turning the pages. 'I also sell a few bottles to friends for the same prices, if you would be interested.'

Oh yes, we would be interested! Even if, as he explained, as private individuals, we had to pay the 21% tax on top of the prices on his lists.

The list was the baseline trade prices for a case of 12 bottles and discounts would be applied for quantity and repeat business by negotiation.

'If you like, I could put a mixed case together for you to try at the prices you see here, plus the tax, of course.'

Yes please!

So I spent a happy hour discussing what Bee and I liked and he cross-referenced that with items in the catalogue while the cat lay on the table and offered helpful comments as she saw fit.

'I'll have it put together for you tomorrow and drop it round after work' explained Graham as he and the cat showed me to the door.

Now that was something to look forward to!

When Graham knocked at our door with a huge box containing our wines it was very hot, and we invited him through to sit on our terrace and get his breath back.

Of course we had to offer him something to drink, so I asked if he would like a glass of wine and if he would prefer red or white.

'Cold,' he said, 'I'm not bothered what it is so long

as its cold!'

Unfortunately the beer I had in the fridge had only just gone in and was still warm, and the only chilled bottle of wine we had in was a bottle of pink plonk from the supermarket, which he was bound to turn his nose up at.

There being nothing else, I produced the bottle and apologised for its lack of provenance.

'Well, it can't be that bad, we supply that supermarket, but I don't think we stock that one.' he said.

Opened and poured, the wine was handed round with some trepidation.
After a polite cough as the wine hit the back of his throat, Graham explained that there were some very good rose wines and, while this one was a little 'young', it did hit the spot in terms of being cold.

He was being polite, of course. It tasted like petrol!

We were very impressed by the the quality and price of the wines Graham provided and told several friends about his services.

When they asked if I could get Graham's business card, I asked him to give me a handful to pass on.

'Business cards are in short supply.' He said ' I have none and my boss doesn't like them. It's the crazy way they do business in Spain, but please pass on the company phone number and my name though.'

'Are you on commission?' I asked.

'Yes, why?'

'Well, if people haven't got your card and just call the company, how does the company know you generated the sale, and how do you get to find out if they have made a sale?'

Graham thought about that for a while, and the next time I saw him he told me he had arranged to have some business cards printed containing his mobile phone number and email address at his own expense.

I didn't like to think that the 'crazy way the Spanish did business' would stand in the way of his making his living, or that there was any possibility of his efforts going unrewarded due to any kind of 'oversight' in recording how the sale was made, back at base, especially as we fully expected to be placing a repeat order with him soon!

BOB ABLE

'I NEED A BIKE!'

'**S**ometimes I wonder if *your* brightness control is faulty!' announced Bee.

'I distinctly told you that my iPad screen had gone dim and all you offered was "turn it off and on again"… don't you think I've tried that already?!'

Bee was getting a little frustrated as she struggled to find her comfort zone in her newly found retirement. She needed to be 'doing something', not sitting about, and after an active working life I was not surprised.

'I think I need a bike,' she declared, 'so I can get a bit fitter and go and get fresh bread from the little shop at the bottom of the mountain in the mornings.'

Although I reminded her just how steep the approach road was to our apartment, and the fact that the journey back from the little shop, where admittedly the bread, freshly baked every morning, was delicious, was all up hill; she had made her mind up.

We needed to purchase a bike.

Of course it needed to have lots of gears to stand a chance of getting up the steep roads (flat Norfolk this was not!) and a basket to hold the fresh bread when purchased, but I had to make it clear that she was on her own in this undertaking. There was no way my slowly disintegrating back would be able to cope with cycling, let alone tackling the mountain roads which separated us from fresh bread each day.

My brightness control might need a nudge every now and then, but I was not entirely without knowledge of my limitations.

Bee, however, was not to be put off.
'I like those old fashioned ones with the wicker baskets and sit up and beg frames,' she stated. 'We should get one of those.'
Well fine, but first we had to find a cycle shop. Any cycle shop … and they were not exactly on every high street corner like Halfords in the UK.

The first one we found had a mixture of exotic mountain bikes and racers with four figure price tickets and, round the back, a handful of similar used bikes with three figure price tags. Not at all what we had in mind.

The big supermarket on the outskirts of the nearby town had frankly very ordinary bicycles for what seemed to us extraordinarily high prices.

In the UK you can buy a brand new, perfectly adequate bike for a little over £100, and some of them are even from manufacturers you might have heard of, but in Spain even the modest Chinese machines are nudging £250 and we struggled to find anywhere selling honest to goodness secondhand bikes.

This area is extremely popular with cyclists who clutter the mountain roads in large groups, and there are dozens of cycling clubs for endurance road riders and racers, so you would think it would be easy enough to pick up one of their cast-offs; but apparently not.

The search would have to resume next time we were in Spain, but just to underline how serious she was about this, when we got back to the UK Bee bought a cycle helmet and some items of clothing.

'Well, you can fit them in your case, I'm sure,' she explained, 'You never seem to take much with you, so there is bound to be room for these few bits. They are much cheaper in the UK as well.'

I'm glad she didn't buy an English push bike and expect me to get that in my hand luggage as well!

BOB ABLE

❖ ❖ ❖

'THE JEWEL IN THE CROWN'. AUGUST 2019

We were back in the UK again when I got a letter from the hospital.

One of the perennial problems and causes of dismay and frustration when visiting the English medical profession, is the seemingly endless waiting.

Whether at the local doctor's surgery or hospitals everywhere, the waiting has to be endured; and lately I seem to have had to do more than my fair share of it.

Now, I'm the last to run-down the British National Health Service (they seem to to be able to do that all on their own, without any help from me) and I'm the first to praise the tireless efforts of the doctors and nurses there, despite the tired facilities and sometimes unsatisfactory conditions in which they are expected to work, so I'll just talk about the waiting.

Recently I have had to wait to get appointments to go to doctors, wait to get seen in clinics, and wait to have my height and weight checked again, in case it has altered in the three days since they last checked it. I have waited to see consultants, nurses and receptionists and waited for replies to letters and emails.

Worst of all I have had to wait to get appointments. I'm always having to wait to get appointments, and it never seems to occur to anyone to fix the next appointment when you are actually in the current one.

The UK system dictates you must wait for a letter offering you a time on a day you can't make (although you told them the dates you could not attend last time); wait for them to lose, find, and consult your notes; wait while the people you need to see are on holiday, at lunch, on strike or off sick; and finally wait in a waiting room.

Sometimes you even get to wait in two separate waiting rooms for the same appointment, as you inch closer to your destination.

It is crazy, and the craziest part of it is the habit of sending out appointment letters for several people to attend the same clinic at the same time, on the same day; so that we can all sit in a sort of sickly troop before one by one, and in no discernible order, each of us is called and marches into endure the next part of the process.

I'm told, but I have no personal experience of this, that the Spanish Health Care system is light years ahead of the NHS in this regard and, as you work your way through the system each doctor, consultant or receptionist, before you leave them, calls the next one you need to see and makes your next appointment for you, right then and there.

I have heard that, in the nearby town at least, if you are admitted for an overnight stay to the sparkling quite new hospital, you will normally be given a private room with en-suite facilities, that waiting times are almost inconsequential and that the facilities are as clean as a new pin; or needle, perhaps.

Furthermore I understand that most, if not all, the private rooms have chairs and a pull out bed so that a relative, partner or parent can stay with the patient overnight.
To be fair, I have also heard that it is for those loved ones to bring in food for the patient, although I doubt if that is true.

I do however know that the Spanish system allows for emergency healthcare which is free at the point of use, just like the NHS.

The nurse in the 'pre-operative unit' I had to visit in the UK could offer me nothing positive

about when my procedure might take place when I visited in early August, but did say that there was a "fair possibility" that it would be done before we travelled to Spain,
in mid-October.

That's right, I said *Pre-Operative Unit* (which I was attending for a *pre-operative* assessment, prior to having an operation) and yes, you read correctly that no appointment had been made, or was going to be made to carry out the operation itself!

Most hospitals have missed their cancer treatment time targets so badly and for so long that I suspect some crafty NHS manager had come up with a wheeze to fiddle the figures by inviting patients to a pre-operative assessment, with no idea when the actual procedure could be performed, so that they could demonstrate moving people from one waiting list to another and meet one of their targets. But it was still a waiting list, and I was still waiting.

Finding worthwhile comparisons between countries is hard to come by, but the NHS was revealed to be underperforming their peers in Ireland, Spain and Slovenia in a global ranking.

It managed to achieve equal footing with Cyprus, Qatar and the Czech Republic, but was just 30th in the rankings produced by the highly respected publication 'The Lancet', a medical journal which rated 192 countries in a detailed and thorough report in 2017.

Overall the UK achieved a score of 84.6 out of 100, but with an especially low score for cancer care. This score has improved since 1990 when it achieved 74.3 against its peers, but it is hardly a glowing assessment.

With the UK now lagging behind many of its European neighbours including Finland, Sweden, Italy and Spain, all of whom have very comparable healthcare systems to the NHS, it is a worrying picture; but at least it is better than the USA, which with a score of just 81.3 points puts it in 35th place.

However, on cancer specifically, the NHS performed particularly badly, scoring between 58 and 64 out of 100 for some types of cancer treatment, according to the report.

On the other hand the report ranked Spain as 8th best in the world.

So much for the NHS being the jewel in the British Crown; and not so good for me as I try to navigate the system in the UK.

If it was possible, which of course it isn't, I'd be much better off using the Spanish healthcare system to fight my current ailments, but with the latest pronouncements stating that (real or imagined) legislation was coming out in Spain to insist on a visa being stamped on entering and leaving the country (with payments extracted, of course) and that the maximum stay permitted was to be reduced to 90 days in any one year, things are uncertain once again.

At the time of writing there is of course nothing definite about alterations to the requirements to actually emigrate to Spain or become a 'Tax Resident' there, but rumours abound of the Spanish Authorities procrastinating when Brits apply to join the 'Padron' (which is the equivalent of the Electoral Role in the UK), or apply for 'Residencias' to demonstrate that they live in the country; and of decisions deliberately not being made until Brexit is finally resolved.

If we can only be in Spain for 90 days in any year that will be a shame, but as with anything Brexit related, nothing is certain and we won't know until we know!

In the meantime I shall take my notebook with me to all my hospital appointments in the UK and write about what I see. It will give me something to do while I am waiting!

Hang on; that's all a bit grim and serious.

Keep reading though, you will like the next chapter, it features some adventures of Barkley the dog.....

◆ ◆ ◆

BARKLEY AND
THE BLIND MAN.

After our trip to the 'Festes Major' in the summer it was going to be a while until our next trip to Spain. I would have liked it to be sooner but all the hospital appointments I hoped to attend, or have cancelled on me at the last minute, meant I was stuck in the U.K. for now, so it seemed right to deal with a few neglected issues in our house.

We fixed the bald patch in the lawn, removed the weeds strangling the camellia and put the much loved sports car up for sale as, although we thought it was great, it had only covered 1,000 miles in the last twelve months and there was really no point in keeping it. Better to let someone else enjoy it.

We bought paint for one of the bathrooms and waterproof boots (which leaked) for Bee to walk the dog, given that it was getting beyond me to walk him myself.
We also took another step to try to deal with one

of the annoying little habits of Barkley the dog, by arranging to fit blinds to the window overlooking the road so that he wouldn't be so engaged with barking at any passers by.

Readers of my earlier memoir 'Spain Tomorrow' will recall that Barkley is a peculiar rescue dog with issues.

Sweet and cuddly at home but somewhat difficult to deal with when out and about, this odd little corgi shaped mongrel barks at cyclists, lorries, motorbikes, shopping trolleys, waiters, birds, postmen, neighbours, window cleaners and, of course, tradesmen.

We have known the diminutive Nick for years, and he has fitted carpets and blinds for us in a series of houses each time we moved. This 5'0" dynamo has interests outside his work in weightlifting and 'strongest man' events, but is the mildest mannered and most charming guy you could hope to meet.

We had called him in to measure up for some vertical blinds, but Barkley, of course, was not impressed.

As the van drew up into the driveway it started.

Barkley always announced the arrival of visitors, but this was different. He stood on his short hind legs like a meerkat on the arm of the sofa nearest the window with his hackles up, and gave voice.

Extensively and at volume!

We have no need for a doorbell as Barkley can always be relied upon to set up a hullabaloo when anyone approaches the house, but poor Nick had hardly opened the door of his van before the dog gave it both barrels.

The problem is that Barkley was at the front of the queue when they handed out the really deep, loud, aggressive sounding barks and despite only being little and actually quite timid, the noise he makes ensures he is much misunderstood.

We got him from the Dog's Trust charity in a 're-maindered sale' and we knew he had problems.
He had been badly mistreated and barked (and barked) as a defence mechanism.
And because his bark is at least twice as big as he is, he believes his strategy works and is reluctant to change it, no matter how we might want him to!

Nick likes dogs, and always made a fuss of our previous labradors, but Barkley objected to him for some reason and insisted on being heard.

It is in a corgi's nature to herd things (they were originally bred to herd cattle) and, perhaps because of his size, Barkley decided that Nick was the ideal candidate to be herded, and he chased the poor man around the lounge and dining room, nudging the back of his legs as he tried to measure up the windows for blinds.

In the end Bee admonished him in her best teacher's voice and he was banished to the garden as Nick quietly breathed a sigh of relief.

I'm not sure whether Nick was disappointed when we accepted his quote for the blinds but, on the day they were to be fitted we all hoped the weather would be fine, so that Barkley, equipped with a new rawhide bone perhaps, could be shut out in the garden to work out his frustrations on his own!

◆ ◆ ◆

On the list of repairs and work to be done on our UK home there was some fencing and tree work to do.

The previous year Barkley had been poisoned by eating berries which fell into our garden from a very straggly and over grown Hawthorn at the end of a neighbour's garden. Vet bill aside, money had to be spent to remove this nasty thing before it happened again, and I approached our neighbour about resolving the issue.

Repairs were required to some fencing, which of course we, rather than the neighbour owned according to the deeds of the house, and there were also trees to be pruned in our own garden.

Our neighbour is a sprightly retiree who over the

years has built up a small portfolio of houses, including the bungalow with the offending tree, which he rented out. He explained that the bungalow was currently empty, awaiting a new tenant, so there would be no problem if we wanted to remove the tree and replace the fences, unless, of course, we wanted him to contribute anything towards the cost. Although the tree was his he made it clear that if we wanted anything done about it, any cost was down to us.

I had rather thought that might happen and, resigned to bearing the full fiscal pain myself, with his agreement, I arranged for fencers and tree surgeons to give me quotes.

That is how I came to be in touch with the 'Top Notch Countryman', or so it said on the side of his van.

I'd know of this wild-haired and somewhat eccentric chap for some years and knew he did tree work along with things like hedging and ditching for local landowners and a few smaller fry like me.

He really is a true countryman and, when not working, can be seen in the woods of the next village riding his massive horse bareback with a falcon on his arm, or flying nearby, and his dog in hot pursuit.

He had spent some years working on a nature conservation project and knew the proper names of plants and trees, and all about wildlife habitat management. He is one of those fiercely clever misfits who embarrass us all with their knowledge of the countryside and zest for life.

He shares his house, which he probably whittled himself from a dry stick and two Boy Scouts, with a menagerie which to my knowledge includes various birds of prey, including several hawks, and a Barn Owl which he raised from an egg when it's parents nest was disturbed. There are also some horses, rabbits, chickens and dogs. There may be more, but not having been invited to his secluded house in the woods, I cannot be certain.

I am, however, sure that there must be frogs, living in a substantial pond, because he informed me that spring was much too early this year and the frogs, who breed 'reg'lar as clockwork', on the 12th March in a normal year, were at it already and keeping him awake with their racket!

I accepted his very reasonable quote for the tree work and agreed with is assessment that the offending Hawthorn was in fact the last remnant of a hedgerow, long since removed, which hadn't been properly pruned or cut back for decades.

I also liked his suggestion that if we simply reduced the trunks to about a metre and a half above the ground, it would recover and the little birds could still use it to nest but would not, as now, be scared away by the bigger birds who currently used it as a perch.

It was all very plausible and I called my neighbour to explain and ask his permission to proceed.

Having received his consent, and a reminder that he wasn't paying for it, I arranged the dates for the work to be done.

When the day came for the 'Top Notch Countryman' to start he arrived, fashionably late, and started to lay out his harnesses, ladders and tools. I made him coffee and discussed the work.

It was something of a surprise when he asked me if I would mind if his Harris Hawk, complete with perch, could come into the garden while he worked.

This, he explained, was a young bird which he needed to get used to humans and, tethered as it was, it would sit quietly while he worked.

'Perhaps I'll leave Barkley inside, though,' I said, 'I don't want him eating him!'

"It's a she, and she won't eat your little dog." He replied, completely failing to spot my pathetic joke.

Although when the fearsome bird came out of the van and was introduced to the garden, I was not so confident, and made sure Barkley was securely locked in the house!

We chatted about this and that as more coffee was drunk between bouts of sawing and clipping and I learned to appreciate what a great depth of country lore this unusual countryman had.

He stuck to his price despite my adding the removal of a small conifer to the list of work and, loading the bird back into its transit box in the van, with a chick as a reward he started to clear up his equipment.

An encounter with such an interesting and knowledgeable man is a rare pleasure indeed, and it is to be hoped that the skills and empathy he has with the countryside and nature will not be lost.

As he finished clearing up his tools, without a word he went and got a large leaf blower from the van and, using a few bits of scrap plastic netting he found behind the shed, he created a corral and blew all our (shamefully un-swept) leaves from the bottom of the garden into it.

'There,' he said, 'That hedgehog you've got living under there will enjoy that, I think!' and without another word he put the leaf blower away.

Rural Norfolk is the richer for giving this individual and others like him the space to persue his alternative lifestyle. I am looking forward to our conversations when I shall be calling him back next year, and there will be more coppicing and pruning to be done.

THE RAIN IN SPAIN

At last it was time to travel to Spain again, and this time we were due at Southend Airport to experience the delights of an Easy Jet flight.

We had never flown from Southend before, but, in the month that the huge Thomas Cook travel empire folded, it offered reasonably priced flights and long term parking so we took the plunge.

However, the long term off site parking we booked was bizarre and without Sat-Nav we would never have found it. Although it was run by a well known company with facilities at many airports, for Southend they had elected to hide their operations away on a sprawling and slightly seedy industrial estate. Having handed over our keys so the car could be parked (which we never like doing, given all the stories you hear about cars being parked on residential roads and used and bashed about by careless handlers) we were expected to wait for the mini-bus in a rickety timber and plastic structure, open to the elements on one side, next to the 'Portacabin' which served as an office.

With only a rough timber bench to sit on, comfortable it was not!

Still, at least they got us to the airport in good time for our flight to Alicante where, on landing in a torrential downpour the pilot, to multiple groans, announced

"Well, as you see, the rain in Spain falls mainly on the plane!"

and went on to explain that we had not been allocated an 'airgate' (the caterpillar like flexible tube that connects to the aircraft doors and ensures passengers can embark or disembark in the dry) and would be expected to walk to the terminal.

Fortunately the kindly Spanish airport operators took pity on us and sent out an enormous bus. It had few seats but plenty of straps and handles to hold as defence against the fierce brakes and jolting swaying motion of the no doubt overloaded vehicle. It rapidly took us to the terminal, allowing us to dismount under cover of the main building, for which we were very grateful.

As ever, Claus Parking, our much preferred airport parking provider in Alicante had washed our car and checked the tyre pressures when they released it from the enormous warehouse where it lived undercover when we were not using it in Spain.

The second rain water rinse nature provided did it no harm and having collected the keys from the little office and been greeted by the resident cat, who sleeps contentedly in an 'in tray' on the desk when not overseeing the work of the delightful and ever helpful staff, we were on our way.

It was late when we arrived at our apartment, but a cursory glance showed all to be in order and, after a few restorative deep breaths on the terrace and observing that the rain had not troubled our property, we headed for bed.

It was good to be back and I was ready for a peaceful and enjoyable break.

Life frequently surprises me, but on our second day back in Spain it caught me out again.
In return for a free advertisement for my first book in this series, Spain Tomorrow, I had agreed to deliver a copy of the book to the editor of the local e-newsletter.

On the way we visited Miguel and Gabriela, the

proprietors of our favourite local cafe/bar at the base of the mountain for lunch, and I cheekily asked them to display a poster advertising the book.

To my surprise they were already aware of my efforts and were anxious to actually buy a copy of the book themselves. Delighted and very flattered by their kind comments I immediately gave them the copy of the book destined for the editor of the e-newsletter so that we had to return to the apartment to pick up another one before I could fulfil my promise.

When we found the development she lived on, Pat greeted us with a call as we rounded the corner of her property trying to spot the numbers on the doors.

"Are you Bob?" she called "Come on in!"

We sat with Pat and her charming Austrian neighbour on her terrace and exchanged pleasantries and discussed the charms of the surrounding district.

Unlike the UK, where we always talk about the weather; here, where the weather can generally be relied upon to be pretty fabulous, the standard introductory topic is usually a polite discussion about the delights of the location and local attractions.

When the conversation turned to business, to my absolute surprise, Pat asked me to sign her copy of the book and add a little dedication! I had never before been asked for such a thing and was momentarily unsure what to do.

Bee explained that this was to be a first for me and, while my face flamed red in embarrassment, I blustered and made a meal of searching for a pen.

It was the most flattering moment I have had since first attempting to publish a book, and if it ever happens again I shall be better prepared with a pen close at hand!

GRANDMA AND THE MENU

We travelled to Denia and stopped for a light lunch (a little tapas) one sunny day. The bar we chose was quite close to the sea and the port and therefore in the area where tourists felt most at home in this town.

It seemed our neighbours at an adjacent table were not feeling at home at all, though.
There was Grandma, Son and Daughter-in-Law, sitting with Auntie who seemed to be in charge.

They struggled with the menu and Auntie was on an app on her phone to translate.
"What's a bocadillo?" Grandma said, "I'm not eating that, I just want a sandwich and some lemonade."

Grandma, it emerged was a diabetic and on this, her first trip to Spain, had not eaten anything at all today, having refused "That muck" for breakfast in the hotel. She was getting tetchy.

"If she don't eat somethink soon she'll pass out." said Daughter-in-Law.

"I dunno what jamón is," said Son.
"It's chicken, innit?" offered Daughter-in-Law in the strident tones of her London home.

"God knows," said Son waving the menu, "All I know is Mum said to make Grandma eat suffink. How about some chips?"

"What's allitas?" Auntie was searching her phone app again.

I felt for Grandma, she was very obviously becoming more and more agitated and was uncomfortable at their table, which was in the full sun.
As they ordered Coca Cola, on the basis that it was all they recognised, I could hold back no longer and decided to offer my help.

My own mother had been diabetic and I recognised the distress the old lady was feeling; so when Auntie turned again to her phone app and said,
"So what are these allitas then?" I replied,
'Chicken wings. Not much meat on them usually.'

The conversation at their table stopped.

"Coo! You English? Thanks mate."

'Can I help?' I offered.

"We just want some sandwiches," said Son.

'Try bocadillos. They are likely to be baguettes rather than English style sandwiches, but probably as near as you are going to get.'

"Oi can't eat baguettes!" spluttered Grandma "Not wif moi teeth!"

Son and Auntie obviously wanted to persevere with the menu, but the rest of the party had decided against and, while the young Spanish waitress did her best, she was not going to succeed beyond selling them some drinks.

As they fussed over their drinks and decided that pretty much all of the menu was beyond them, they decided to leave, and Auntie approached our table as they gathered their bags and prepared to move on.

"Sorry about that. First time in Spain, you see. And first time abroad for Grandma and she ain't happy. We need to get her to eat somefink because she is diabetic."

'You could try jamón York, patatas y huevos,' I offered, 'That is near as you will get outside the English tourist areas to ham egg and chips.'

"Coo! Thanks." said Son "Oi just fancy that, or a hamburger!"

I did feel sorry for them. This is not tourist central, and ham egg and chips, or for that matter 'full

English breakfast' or 'Sunday roast with gravy' do not feature on the menu round here. In Benidorm, an hour and a half down the motorway, it would be different, but this part of the coast is where the Spanish go on holiday, and that tends to be reflected in the food offered.

"Hamburgers!" muttered Grandma "I ain't eating that muck! Thats what they make with the sweepings off the butcher's floor!"

Auntie rolled her eyes and offered me a wave as they disappeared round the corner.

PARTY!

In the nearby town there is one of those typical narrow streets with restaurants and a chaos of tables all over the roadway.

Other than a shop selling bangles and, incongruously, one selling kitchen wares, this little street is wall to wall cafes and restaurants, with only a narrow gap to walk between the sprawling tables on the roadway. This is no place for cars and the street is shut to traffic.

We have explored a good proportion of the eating houses on this street but, as some seem to open at less convenient times, we have not been in them all yet.

They do all seem to follow broadly the same pattern, however. Offering menu-del-dia or tapas and a more substantial menu at lunchtime and in the evenings for those who require it.

We have a couple of favourites in this street which, while the al-fresco eating option is always tempting, also have pleasant internal spaces, often delightfully decorated and with blissful and very welcome air conditioning.

We found ourselves inside one of these establishments in a nicely cooled courtyard behind the main building on one occasion, and were shown to a table not far from from what turned out to be a teenage birthday party of roughly eighteen young people aged between about 14 and 16 in full swing.

It quickly reached full volume as the burgers were demolished and the girls started their endless trips to the loo in pairs and to the mirror on the wall outside to primp, take selfies and giggle.

The boys sat about in groups or moved around the large table and good-naturedly teased or stole each others chips; and the birthday boy at the head of the table was surprised when the restaurant owner brought out a large and very sticky birthday cake and lit the solitary candle.

The rendition of 'Happy Birthday', in Spanish of course, but to the familiar tune was a delightful interlude, and the young people, although occasionally quite loud, did not misbehave at all.
Apart from occasional visits from the restaurant staff, they seemed to have no adult accompaniment or supervision.

As they filed out at the end of their meal, the last straggler looked over to us and wished us '*buen provecho*' (have a pleasant meal) before departing with a smile.

It would be interesting to speculate whether British children of this age would be allowed out in such a group at 9:30 p.m., in centre of town, on their own and apparently unsupervised.

Although the group were a little loud and obviously excitable, they never-the-less did not upset the other diners, and the whole occasion was rather sweet.

The birthday cake looked good too!

On one occasion, before she retired, Bee had to return to the UK early and, as I was on my own, our friends, Peter and Holly, very kindly took me under their wing.

I am very fond of Peter and Holly and was pleased when, one sultry afternoon, I was invited to join them on a trip out for lunch. We could go, they said, to a rather good little place they had found in Javea, a seaside town about half an hour's drive away, on the other side of the mountain.

Although they had not been to this particular place for a few years, they felt the need to re-acquaint themselves with it and invited me to share the experience.

Peter drove us to Javea and, respecting the fact that I walk with a stick, did his best to find a parking space somewhere near our destination in the crowded and busy old town. After a through investigation of the narrow streets, but with no success, we ended up in an underground carpark a little distance away and had to walk up a steep road to join the very narrow souk like streets where, Peter explained, the restaurant was just around the corner.

After zig-zagging our way ever upwards in the tight, but surprisingly not traffic free lanes, and after a brief look round the indoor market, which was in the process of closing for the day, we paused to get our bearings.

As we admired the enormous ornately carved but battle scarred church doors, Peter announced we were nearly there.

Several of the narrow lanes were being dug up and

worked on for reasons which were not clear and we had to skirt round various holes in the road, builders vans and barriers to continue on our way, accompanied by the sound of jack hammers and cement mixers. But the minor diversions seemed to cause a problem.

'Its up there, isn't it?' asked Holly.

"No, I think its down that street," said Peter, setting off at his usual brisk pace as we scuttled after him, casting wistful glances all the while at the fine looking bistros and bars we passed with their enticing cooking smells.

Two lanes and one dead end later, in the middle of some more areas being dug up and cordoned off, beside an enormous yellow digger, Peter stopped and announced that we had arrived.

As we caught up however, it was obvious that the bistro, sitting on its own in an otherwise mainly residential little street, was closed; and by the look of it, it had been shut for some time!

Peter looked crestfallen, but I had noticed that, at the end of the lane, we could see the road which led down to the car park, only a little further down the hill.

'Shall we go to one of the other places we passed instead?' I said.

"Time's getting on," Holly added, "They will be shutting the kitchens soon!"

'I don't fancy all this dust and building work,' said Peter, looking around at all the builder's debris, 'Let's get out of here.'

So we headed back to the car.

We drove to another area of the town but again failed to find anywhere to park, and we drove round two surface car parks looking for a space in vain.

'Is Javea always this busy?' I asked.

Holly raised her eyes to heaven, "Only at this time of year!" she said.

'This is dreadful,' grumbled Peter as we waited for yet another hire car driver to decide which exit on the roundabout his Sat-Nav wanted, 'Let's call it a day here!'

Eventually we ate in a more traditionally Spanish

place we had visited before, beside the main road, two miles from Peter and Holly's home. Luckily we just got our order in before they closed the kitchens.

My introduction to touristy Javea old town had been brief and dusty but, ever intrepid, Peter vowed that we would try again another time.

"And perhaps set off a bit earlier, next time!" added Holly.

The Spanish tend to eat lunch at around 2:00 p.m. or maybe a little later, but perhaps in the more tourist focussed places they move this feast forward to cater for British habits.

We have visited Javea many times since this little excursion and throughly enjoyed ourselves in digger free streets, or by the immaculate beaches.

Clearly excavations on the otherwise charming lanes climbing out of the old town might take place at any time, although I wondered if all the bustle, drilling and determined industry by the builders on that first occasion, which seemed to take no account of diners or passers-by, was simply to get the work done before that immovable traditional Spanish institution; Siesta time!

THE CAT IS IN CHARGE. OCTOBER 2019.

E arly in our October visit we made contact with Graham the Wine Merchant and invited him over. He arrived with an excellent bottle of wine as a gift and, as we opened the door, 'Silke' his delightful and highly talkative little black cat, shot past him and began exploring our apartment as if she owned the place!

With an appreciative 'mew' as we sat down to cheese, olives and thin slices of quite highly spiced Ibérico ham, she hopped onto my lap and made it clear that she would like to try a portion.

Despite being quite spicy, after obtaining Graham's permission, I offered her a slice of the ham and to everyone's surprise she took it delicately, hopped down and devoured it with relish under the table.

Graham told us how this remarkable little cat, a

former stray, had accompanied him on intercontinental road trips, sitting unrestrained on the passenger seat of his car, walked happily on a lead and was without doubt quite a character. She did not, however, normally like spicy food, ignored cheese and was something of a fussy eater, so when she made no bones about asking for a second slice of the ham, Graham expressed his surprise.

Whilst she made herself comfortable on a red cushion on one of our sofas and eyed us with interest, Graham sold us on some of the latest wines he had discovered and, three bottles down, we had placed an order for more supplies.

After a pleasant evening sitting on the terrace with wine glasses in hand, as he prepared to leave, Graham produced a handful of business cards, freshly printed with his contact details and asked if I would mind passing them around a few of my friends. With these to hand Graham would be less likely to miss out and would be sure to get his commission this time, if a sale resulted.

Despite a somewhat insistent 'morning head' the next day, when Graham arranged to deliver our latest order, I realised that we had got rather carried away and we would need further wine racks to accommodate it all. At least there was no danger of our dying of thirst!

The little cat accompanied him again as he

brought over the boxes full of wine bottles that evening but, after a cursory inspection, left in disgust when it became obvious that no further slices of spiced ham were to be provided!

After that the little cat became a regular visitor and was often waiting outside our front door to dash inside and make herself at home on the terrace in the sun or, if we were going out, under one of the beds, from where we had to coax her out if we were unable to entertain her due to prior commitments.

If we were passing when Graham had gone to work, she would often greet us on the steps up to our property with a series of mews and chirrups. She had clearly decided that we were acceptable as surrogate minions to provide her with comfort when required.

Graham made a special trip to buy some of the spiced ham she had enjoyed so much, but of course, being a cat, when he offered it to her she turned her nose up and strutted away without touching it!

The business cards were more successful, however, and one I gave to the delightful bar owner in the market produced an instant response and an order for Graham, with the promise of more to come; so we felt we had earned our bottle of wine!

WATER EVERYWHERE, BUT NONE TO DRINK!

The rain in Spain also falls on our apartment on occasions, and sometimes in massive torrents known as 'Gota Fria'.

Although, by all accounts we had missed the worst of it, further south, around the Segura river, much damage was done to property and persons when it burst its banks.

When a second event was threatened, to coincide with our visit in October, we were grateful that it came to nothing much, with only a day and a night of solid rain to contend with.

This time the effects were no more than inconvenient, although the road tunnel under the the little coastal railway line at the bottom of 'our' mountain was impassable for some days and filled with muddy water washed from the golf course to a depth of about four feet.

The Gota Fria was not the only water related incident we encountered in October, however. Late on one warm Saturday afternoon we noticed that our taps had run dry and we had no water supply.

Normally the water supply is very reliable but enquiries of our neighbours revealed that the problem was ours alone and we could find no reason for it.

We checked that we had paid the bill and on confirming that we had, we decided to wait to see if it was just a temporary thing and if it would fix itself. It didn't of course, and 24 hours later, on a Sunday, with no change in the situation we realised that something had to be done, so I visited our nearest neighbour to ask for help.

I asked in halting Spanish if they would mind calling the 24hr. emergency service number on my mobile phone; but needless to say there was just a recorded message to say call back during office hours during the working week ... thank goodness it wasn't a flood!

The situation was getting quite serious, but I had remembered that down by the larger of the two pools there was a shower with a tap and hose which the pool cleaner used, and I set off to to see if I could fill a bucket with water so that we could at least flush the loo.

My route took me past the balcony of another apartment where I noticed activity. I called up to enquire if the occupant spoke English and, with relief, was greeted by a broad Scottish voice from above.

In the short conversation that ensued I established that Duncan, for that was his name, had no problems with his water supply and that very kindly he would bring us a 'pail o water' and see if he could help.

By this time our Spanish neighbours were up and about and joined the conversation as we endeavoured to find the problem, but Duncan, who had owned his property for 17 years, knew what he was about and undid the wing nut on the bolt which held shut the door of a large service cabinet beside the road to reveal a tangle of pipes and meters.

'Ah wonder...' he muttered as he examined the pipework. 'Open a tap in yer apartment,' he instructed 'and wull soon see!'

The stairs to the adjacent building where work had been going on during the last week or so were covered in a liberal coating of cement dust and the builders debris around had given Duncan pause for thought.

As he rummaged in the service cupboard and located what he was looking for, he said

'Thus here is your main water pipe, and thus are your meters ... If ah can just ... ' and with a grunt he reached in and turned a little tap above the pipe marked with the number of our apartment.

Bee appeared at the front balcony doors "Its running!" she called down.

'Wull turn it off quick while the system refills and look for leaks!' exclaimed Duncan breathlessly, to the sound of rushing water in the pipes.

A short while later Duncan declared that the system had re-filled and we checked and found that all our taps functioned again as normal.

'Your aqua ees turn off?' chipped in Marie. 'Have choo made enemies?'.

I hoped that I had not and looked to Duncan for an explanation.

'Ah think they builders turned off your water instead of the supply to yon place they are working on when they went hame!'

Mystery solved!

Later, and freshly showered, with the help of Google Translate, I composed a note asking that nobody should turn off our water except in an emergency and stuck it on the wall in the cabinet above 'our' pipework.

The builders had made an honest mistake as the apartment they were working on had the same number as ours, but was in the other small adjacent block; but I was anxious not to let it happen again!

Duncan was packing up to leave when I next drove past his allotted space in the garage. I said thank you once more for his help, of course, and received his smiling admonishment for the 'unnecessary' bottle of wine I left on his doorstep. I breathed a sigh of relief once again that we have such wonderful helpful neighbours; especially as Marie had explained that, had we been able to contact them, a call out from the water service people on a Sunday was likely to work out very expensive indeed.

Although the solution was simple in the end, we would have faced a considerable bill (and not a little embarrassment once the cause was established) if not for all their kindness.

INTO THE MOUNTAINS

G raham the Wine Merchant was full of surprises and seemed to lead a charmed life.
He was excellent company and was kind enough to invite us to join him on a trip high into the mountains in his powerful Mercedes, ostensibly to deliver some wine to a client, but also to have lunch at the amazing James Bond film worthy Coll De Rates, high above Parcent and, at 630m above sea level, looking over lesser mountains to the blue Mediterranean on the horizon.

But before we got to this fascinating eyrie, Graham took us to another mountain hideaway to deliver several cases of wine.

Bodega Inn Masserof is an unexpected mix of architectural salvage, museum, ancient buildings and apparently amazing entertainment.

Once a Roman villa, and converted in the 11th Century by the Moors to serve as an 'alqueria' or farmstead, it seems to have been abandoned by the 18th Century but the Bodega winery was re-built in 1972 by English architect Peter Pateman and is now run as a riotous restaurant by his daughter Carolina Pateman-Ivars.

Although we were not to experience the joyous revelry which takes place here first hand, Graham's description was intriguing.

The main building on the sprawling site was the ancient farmstead, with a mezzanine floor for the family to sleep overlooking an open floor where the beasts bedded down. To one side was a massive blackened fireplace which was originally the cooking area and the source of heat for man and beast alike.

Now there was a slightly more modern kitchen added to one side with a bottled gas fridge and a wood burning stove where all the cooking now took place. Running water came from a tank which was replenished as required by a lorry which had to labour its way up the switchback mountain roads.

Visitors to the Bodega Inn Masserof had to make do without electricity, but on certain privileged weekends (only) they were able to book lunch (only) and be coaxed by the effervescent Carolina to mix eating and drinking with singing to their hearts content.

Apparently all diners had to be prepared to sing as a pre-requisite of enjoying the Medieval delights of dining here.

Decorated with a confusingly miss-matched collection of furniture, the area previously occupied by the beasts is now the dining room. The seating includes battered 'thrones' with highly decorative scrolls and flounces painted in bright colours, which rejoice in the somewhat dubious claim that they came from one of the Borgia's palaces, and hard backless long wooden benches all ranged around a huge solid table.

The dozen or so guests, who must book many months in advance, are plied with some home-made wine for free, or bought in wine if they want to pay extra, and are presented with a huge feast of fittingly Medieval proportions.

Graham told us that the bubbly hostess, who we got to meet, was the daughter of a somewhat eccentric man who collected, and presumably also sold, architectural salvage, much of which he had built into or left lying about his adjacent museum, which one could tour for free. He had also restored the original Bodega to produce a drinkable wine in quantities large enough to serve the thirsty diners.

His larger than life daughter had continued the business with the help of her husband, but had concentrated on the rural restaurant, which we were told now had an international following and although only open for limited hours and hidden away was always fully booked up.

The riotous afternoons the patrons enjoyed there had to be carefully planned as, with no telephone or mobile signal, and given the likely levels of alcohol consumption, one could not simply ring for a taxi; and as the location was so remote, on the side of a steep mountain up winding switchback hairpin infested roads, complete with occasional rockfalls, it was unlikely that taxi firms would be prepared to brave the drive in any event!

Despite its difficult access, lack of facilities and limited opening hours, the Bodega Inn Masserof was extremely popular, and the large bill for the wines delivered by Graham and left with the hostess, attested to its success.

Our lunch stop, however, was to be even higher and on the very top of a different mountain with truly spectacular views, and hearty German influenced food to nourish the weary traveller.

After another hairy drive up ear popping mountain roads, we parked in a stony carpark beside a sheer drop, with no barrier and paused to take in our surroundings.

At 630m above sea level, but still popular with intrepid cyclists, the modest single storey building that comprised the heart of the Coll De Rates restaurant has a huge open terrace on two sides with the most spectacular views down mountain passes and over tiny villages and small towns far below.

The views between steppe farms and woodland eventually open to the glistening sea.

Despite being the very end of October, the weather was kind and warm and there was little wind, so we did not need the fleeces and jumpers Graham had urged us to bring as a precaution. There was a slight mist, or perhaps this high up it was cloud, which precluded decent photography, but it would not have surprised me to see James Bond appearing from the cloud in his Gyrocopter and dropping in for a spot of lunch!

It was breathtaking, but location duly admired we tore our eyes away from the views to look at the menu provided by the smiling waitress, and order tall glasses of Erdinger beer and wine for Bee.

Graham had extolled the virtues of the wild boar stew as we wound our way up the mountain roads and with gambas (prawns) in hot garlic butter for a starter he gave the menu but a cursory glance.

What caught my eye however was 'Gipsy in spicy sauce', which I didn't order as I doubted if I could eat a whole one, despite the bracing mountain air, and Bee and I both ordered lamb shanks with beans.

I elected to try the spicy goulash soup as a starter but Bee, sensibly as it turned out, decided to forgo that course and wait for her lamb.
Huge starters out of the way the main courses were delivered and, served on one of those enormous platters you use for carving the Christmas turkey, was the biggest limb of lamb I have ever seen on a plate!

This beautifully cooked feast could easily satisfy a hungry family of four and at first I thought it was to share with Bee. But then her massive matching plate arrived and it became clear that in this location you were expected to eat a mountain as well as enjoy the views from one!

All three of us were roundly beaten by the size of the task before us and tragically had to send back at least enough meat for a modest supper each.

Graham reminded us that we, on the journey there, had listened to his eulogy on the fabulous apple strudel this establishment was famous for ...

'Don't panic, though,' he said ' I can get them to pack it up for us to take home!'

It was 24 hours before we had enough space to tackle the strudel with its little pot of custard in a polystyrene box. It was just as well that the staff at Coll De Rates had obviously encountered this situation before and were well prepared!

As we wobbled our way back to the car, after Graham had left a wine price list with the owners, so as not to waste the potential for a sale, we took one last look at the amazing view and, to my surprise my phone beeped to say that I had emails.

'Good grief!' I said ' There is a full signal right up here!'

'Ah,' said Graham pointing 'That's probably because of that...' and he drew my attention to a phone mast behind the main building that I had not seen before.

Rural and isolated this place may be but it was certainly not out of touch ... prepared and ideal as a base for Mr Bond's operations, it seems!

We never did find out what 'Gipsy in spicy sauce' was ... perhaps it is the name of Mr Bond's next love interest .... no doubt she will be slightly saucy and bring a little spice to the proceedings!

THE FISHERMAN'S QUARTER

C lose to the port in Denia, where the fishing boats dock each week day and sell their catch in the fascinating market on the quayside, sits the original and ancient fisherman's quarter.

Facing the sea, inevitably the buildings have been taken over by tourist focused bars and restaurants, interspersed with the occasional beachwear shop, but one parallel row back and stepping road by little narrow road towards the looming castle, the buildings take on a different flavour.

The Placa de Sant Antoni is a small traffic free square dotted with palm trees and filled on most days with seats for the three or four bars plying their trade there.
The fare is frankly predictable but the buildings are fascinating.

Ancient 'Gaudi', with its facade raised and rebuilt in render above the elderly warm honey coloured stone, has higgledy piggledy windows at odd heights and tiny, steep and uneven steps down to the most inconvenient convenience around.

Cramped it maybe, but as the clientele sit outside for the most part, the building only really has to accommodate the the bar and a server, and most drinks are collected by the waitress through an open window beside the bar.

This window, and another on the other side of the door have wide cills and two or three barstools are placed among the potted plants. These serve mostly for the proprietor and his associates to watch the goings on, it seems.

The tap room itself is dark with low ceilings, and the building has obviously had to be much adapted to accommodate persons of 21st Century height.

Next to it (and it seems to us owned by the same people) sits Ca Tona, painted in muted blue and this time with higher ceilings on three storeys, with a roof terrace approached by a noisy steel staircase bolted to the antique wall. Here, as in most places, you can sit outside and enjoy tapas or just a drink, and chalkboards on the wall flap in the breeze to advertise what is available.

But look up and around you as you take your seat in this little square and notice the pretty tiled panel on one of the less decorative buildings depicting St. Antoni himself and you might spot, on the grill covering the window below, that offerings of flowers have been pushed into the railings.

This might be the edge of tourist Denia, but the old values are still much in evidence. The modern world soon makes it's presence felt however as on the opposite side of the square lurks a much more up to date form of entertainment, where you can buy expensive and elaborate cocktails. Here is a music bar which gets loud enough to be something approaching a nightclub, when the young set arrive late in the evening.

Take a stroll one further road back away from

the sea and it changes again. The new Magazinos development, recently converted from old warehouses, offers a mix of little food outlets and open air restaurants with glass balconies on the upper floors and a stylish, trendy feel.

Leave that behind and things get a bit more Spanish again when in the narrow street, hugger-mugger with the offices of the electricity company, there sits a bodega and a series of most decorative houses with pretty metal flower be-decked balconies in riotous colours. There is a rather posh pizza restaurant and, quietly situated by the door of a small hotel, the confusingly traditional Amazonas bar.

Here, amongst the potted cactus and rough wooden pallets mounted on the wall supporting trailing ivy and profusely blooming creepers, you can be surprised by a Venezuelan themed menu or just stick to the more traditional Spanish tapas displayed in the glass fronted cabinet on the bar or prepared fresh in the tiny kitchen behind a bead curtain.

The beer here is cheap and stone cold, and the banter around the always busy bar stools, in many different languages, is a delight.

Drag yourself away and turn towards the castle at the end of the street, past the inevitable Chinese emporiums selling everything from pins to patio heaters, and you will shortly be walking alongside a high wall, behind which you might hear the children of the school it enfolds playing. If you turn left here you will soon come to the Marquis de Campo, the main shopping street of the town, dotted with 'proper' restaurants and, towards the sea, shops selling ice cream and frozen yoghurt ... but if you walk instead around two sides of the school, turning right, the corner of the large mustard coloured market building will soon come into sight.

Fancy a look inside? Oh, I think we should!

Approaching from this angle we first encounter the main hall, with its permanent stalls selling first bread, then cheese, olives and Iberico ham, which has been thinly carved and laid in decorative fans for customers to sample. Then there are the riotously colourful vegetable and fruit stalls, with exquisitely and artistically laid out displays in the central isle.

Either side, against the outside walls there are butchers specialising in various meats and yet more cheese shops. In the middle, as a focal point, is a flower seller and one of those lottery ticket sellers so beloved of the Spanish everywhere.

On each of the four corners of the central courtyard there is a little bar, each offering different tapas and with stools occupied, each in their turn, by gregarious market traders and quiet old men in caps, who might possibly be the vegetable growers who provide the stock for the traders.

The noise and colour and the exuberant spectacle of it all has to be experienced and is bound to delight. But we are not done yet.

Still further into the hall past the butchers, some concentrating on sausages or skinned rabbits, with their wares hanging over their heads; some focusing on chicken, while another makes burgers with a little press surrounded by prime cuts of beef and pork; and all providing joints trimmed just as their customers request in beautifully wrapped wax paper parcels; we come at last to the separate fish market.

The enormous pale permanent marble slabs arranged around three walls are angled to display the eclectic mix of the life of the Mediterranean, caught this very day, and some of it still alive.

The pink spider crabs, and spiny blue-black sea urchins sit next to trays of the enormous and very famous Denia prawns, overseen by twitching lobsters, while cuttle fish, squid, octopus, and mussels all await their fate.

The fish range from bright red boxy bodied to tiny little things in rainbow colours interspersed with enormous shark like creatures, conger eels, and the more recognisable cuts of cod, hake, plaice and skate. There are many fish I do not recognise … is that an angler fish being wrapped up?… And many that gaze at the passers by with a malevolent stare, as if in reproach for snatching them from the sea.

Amongst the ice stand white coated red faced fishmongers wielding knives, as the waves of restaurateurs and housewives alike press forward and jostle to examine the catch.

The market men and women work hard to replenish the stock until, all too soon, it is gone, and the market empties until tomorrow.

All, that is, except at the little bars where the traders sit and chat with the handful of locals who are 'in the know' and become bar flies at this time of day.

Bee and I sometimes meet our friends Peter and Holly and several other regulars at Marta's bar in the main hall of the market.

We shouldn't really call it a bar because it is not supposed to be, but Marta has been serving wine and freshly prepared tapas to her customers for so long that nobody really minds.
The pitch is ostensibly selling a wide range of smoked and cured fish products, presented in tins

and bottles, and flavoured cooking salts, relishes and pickles.

The wine and beer are no doubt much more profitable for her, however, and as a meeting point for friends and acquaintances from many nations, this fascinating place stands alone.

Marta is still battling to get permission to have stools for her customers, but the management of the market won't hear of it. They insist that she is a shopkeeper, not a bar owner, but although like everyone else they have to stand, the market managers still come and have a glass of wine leaning on the bar ... I mean counter ... when the mood takes them!

One of the attractions is that the wine served here is of excellent quality and, thanks to some rapid business card work on my part, is occasionally provided by Graham the Wine Merchant.

During the short period the Ruta de Tapas is running restaurants and bars provide a drink and a tapa for three euros, but at Marta's bar you can get generally superior wine and a tapa for that price all year round!

Marta speaks excellent English and, when not sailing her boat, sometimes gives Peter and Holly Spanish lessons. She also did her best to find Bee a secondhand pushbike on the local internet sites and is always a most welcoming hostess.

It's a bit far for Bee to ride her newly acquired bike to the market, although the basket on the front would be invaluable for transporting all the little goodies from her stock that Marta tempts us with, so we have to moderate our intake and drive into Denia, but we love visiting the market generally and with a warm welcome always waiting at Marta's bar, we are very regular visitors.

RUTA DE TAPAS.

Here in Spain at this time of year, in nearby Denia, we can indulge in the wonderful Ruta de Tapas or Tapas Trail.
It is a delightful event held every year which involves up to 40 of the local hostelries offering, in return for a modest €3, a glass of wine, beer or vermouth and a really special tapa. This little morsel is designed to advertise their culinary expertise both visually and in terms of taste. It is their annual chance to showcase their skills in the hope of attracting punters to visit again for something more substantial.

By November 2nd, eight days after this particular Ruta de Tapas started, we had visited 18 restaurants and tried the little offerings they presented us with enthusiastically.
That is at least eighteen glasses of wine each!

Not all were to our taste, of course, and one or two, whilst inventive to look at, did not hit the mark as a tempter to try a full meal. Indeed one was so small it barely filled the cup indentation on the espresso saucer it was served on. It didn't taste that great either.

It was served with a mean drizzle of very ordinary wine in a flat bottomed glass (the sort of thing you put tea-lights in), so really it was a canapé with a shot of wine and as such it missed the point entirely.

That is not to say all the restaurants were mean in their offerings, and one or two were truly outstanding. One was very substantial and almost a full meal in itself!

Each was due to be judged and the winner would be awarded a coveted trophy, and there was a host of runner up prizes. The little book participants were issued with had a section to mark each tapa, out of five, on three categories:-

Degustacion
Creatividad
Servicio

Each establishment stamped the little book as we went round and each place was out to prove their mettle. The rivalry between them was intense.

There was also a prize for the customers, who, if they returned the little book with the official stamps of at least 15 establishments, would be entered in a draw for attractive prizes too... With 18 out of the 40 restaurants visited we were eligible to enter, and although we had no chance of getting round all 40 places on the list in the time available to us, we were determined to try to get round as many as possible.

It wasn't exactly hard work (except perhaps for the liver) and was certainly great fun!

We were due to travel back to England on the 7th November, so we thought we had better get a move on with all these little tapas places, and try as many as we could.

We had started at Ca Toña in Placa Sant Antoni, which is more bar than restaurant, so we weren't expecting much, but the little bowl of broad beans with Iberico ham, a sliced quails egg, little bits of toast doused in olive oil and herbs (advertised as being from the Sierra de Mariola) was very tasty, and hid a surprise in the form of a few tiny pieces of crystallised fruit to sweeten it up. It was very pleasant.

Round the corner was Movida Denia where there was some confusion when we ordered the Ruta de Tapas dish as the waiter, working solo, had obviously not been prepared for the eventuality of people ordering these dishes. It took an age to come, most of which seemed to be taken up with the somewhat embarrassed waiter making frantic phone calls and trying to call up reinforcements. Similar confusion reigned when we came to pay as the waiter explained that the complicated looking computerised till had not yet been set up to recognise this dish and he didn't know how to record the sale. In the end I left the money and let them sort it out.

When it did eventually appear the dish itself was a much bigger portion than one normally associates with tapa, and I suspect was larger than they should have served. It comprised some 'morcilla' or black pudding (but more finely minced than we are used to in the U.K. and not so fatty) with a slice of caramelised baked apple topped with a cheese wafer and some miniature flowers and fresh herbs. It was very pretty, but not to Bee's taste, so I got to finish hers.

I suspect that, in his confusion, the waiter also served us a much larger glass of wine (which he topped up to make up for the delay) than was planned. The wine was good, too!

Next up was the newly opened Taberna Senieta, where frankly the wine was awful. But there were real compensations in that the tapa, a little morsel of chickpea and rosemary with a sweet onion and creamed cod sauce, deep fried in batter, was absolutely delicious and delightfully presented.

This small restaurant, which stands on its own in the Calle Senieta, had literally just opened for business after extensive repairs to the fabric of the building and, as we were the only customers, we got chatting, in a mix of English, Spanish and hand gestures, with Cara one of the three owners.

The conversation turned to wine and without being rude about what she was serving, the opportunity arose for me to produce one of Wine Merchant Graham's business cards. It appeared she was going to need it, and she arranged for Graham to go and see her the next day and, when it runs out, to replace the nasty wine they bought from a local Bodega with something a bit more palatable. This little place had a very different menu and Cara explained that it would change everyday depending on what she bought fresh from the fishing boats early each morning. This close to the port it was unsurprising that the menu featured a lot of fish, but Cara obviously knew what she was doing when buying it as turbot and other rarities featured on the chalkboard on the day we visited.

Each time we walked past Taberna Senieta from that point Cara always gave a wave or made time for a little chat with us. It was one we were happy to visit again, and when we did the wine was much better!

The market was our next destination where we ordered the Ruta de Tapas dish at La Lateria, or as we know it Marta's bar and there we stopped to gather ourselves for our next attempt to try new places tomorrow.

Whilst it is also possible to visit the restaurants on the Ruta de Tapas in the evening, and indeed at least one was not open at lunchtime, we decided to restrict our explorations, to give our livers a chance to recover, to daytime visits.

Next on our list was a really decorative tapa from a very ordinary looking cantina (cafe) where the Spanish clientele lingered over coffee, tostada (toast, sometimes with tomato and olive oil) and cigarettes late into the morning.

'Havannah', on the Calle la Via, had little to recommend it at first glance and was positioned on the shady side of the wide street near a children's play park. Other than on the occasions when these streets fill with processions, when a stage is erected to be used by a live band during one of the festivals and fiestas, this quiet street is away from the action and 'Havannah' is surrounded by a mixture of offices, flats and secondary shops.

We had visited before with friends who lived very nearby for an ordinary snack lunch, but other than that it was not a place we had paid much attention to.

The expression 'never judge a book by its cover' came to mind as the unsmiling waitress delivered the most amazing looking tapa to our table outside.

Entitled 'Flamencura', in the little book used to describe each dish, this one was visually stunning... and tasted good too!

The description of what we were to eat appeared in the book as follows...
"Pastel de patata, ibérico con aroma de albahaca y solomillo en salsa de boletus al oporto"
Basically, that's a potato cake with basil and a piece of sirloin in a port sauce. As the picture shows, it was far more elaborate than that!

Over the following days we visited many more places and enjoyed all sorts of little treats.
The little pillow of puff pastry stuffed with a tasty stew in the Txoko Bar (pronounced 'chocko', we are given to understand) was so good I had two!

The ordinary looking piece of toast with a spoon

of warm Iberico ham casserole and a fried egg at Toma Jamon in the Calle Diana looked nothing, but was one of the best we had in terms of flavour.

Further along the same street at a bar I'd better not name, the cold mashed cod in a glass was revolting, and we left it.

Also in a glass, over a brandy sauce, a ball of morcilla in breadcrumbs hovered on a stick balanced across the rim at Res Que Tapas in Plaza del Convento. We decided it was just plain strange.

Then again the ordinary looking 'slider' (a miniature burger in a small bun) at 'Pointer' on Plaza Maria Pineda was much enjoyed and went down as one of Bee's favourites.

La Traviesa on Calle La Via doesn't look much from the outside, and neither did the little pot of venison goulash they provided, but it tasted absolutely fabulous and I had to be dragged away before I could order another.

In the newish La Glorieta restaurant, in addition to its regular and quite pricy menu, their Ruta de Tapas offering was a few tasty prawns in garlic with sun-dried tomato on a little coca (small pizza base). It was pleasant to sit by the fountain in the little circular garden area opposite the bar with walls and pillars draped with prolifically flowering bougainvillea.

As you can see from the picture, one of the highlights visually was the so called 'Dulce O Salado' from La Cova Talla on Calle Loreto, which is a restaurant we like anyway.

But El Convent, in Plaza del Convento had taken their eye of the ball a bit in terms of making their tapa attractive. It was simply a hot dog in a little roll with mustard and tomato ketchup. It tasted OK but it was a bit ordinary.

In the Marquis de Campo, Bavaria Brau's effort however was absolutely stunning, both visually and to taste, with a clever wafer made of cheese, and featuring apple cream and once again the morcilla (but this time better flavoured). It was the first time Bee admitted that she had enjoyed one of the black pudding dishes.

There were too many others to record, and if I'm honest, the wine haze was starting to confuse the memory by the first few days of November. But what I can say is that if you are passing when the Ruta de Tapas is on, do dive in and try it. It is great fun.

❖ ❖ ❖

SUNDAY LUNCH

There is a little electric passenger ferry, powered by sunlight generated by the solar panels that form its roof, in Denia harbour.

It shuttles the short distance between the town side of the water and the outer harbour area which contains upmarket bars and restaurants and the dock for the Ibiza ferry; and it is free to use.

Although it is perfectly possible to walk around the spit of land that encloses the harbour, it is fun to ride on this little boat and admire the half-dozen luxurious 'super-yachts' that moor there, and the flow of little boats passing to and fro. The ferry is much in demand and always busy.

The last time we used it to travel from the outer harbour to the town, we were accompanied by a couple of families with excitable children, complete with bikes and scooters, obviously out for the traditional weekend get together before lunch.

The weather was delightful as we pressed the little button to call the ferry (although there was no need as it we could see it was taking on passengers on the other side of the bay) and initially we were the only people on our side waiting.

However we were soon joined by three generations of a large family, all smartly dressed and ranging in age from the elderly matriarch, clutching a vast handbag, to the tiniest baby, clutching his mother's bold necklace.

As father stood to one side and discussed important matters with the other men, mother and an older daughter attempted to corral the younger children in the waiting area and keep those with wheeled transport away from the steep boarding ramp that leads down to the water, where there are no barriers to prevent a dunking.

Another slightly smaller family joined us with older children who immediately started to play with the original family as the men exchanged greetings with those already engaged in discussions on matters of the day.

By the time the ferry docked and started to disgorge it's passengers, we had been joined by another middle aged couple and some slightly uncomfortable looking younger adults, who were obviously tourists and did not join in the joyous hubbub created by those already on the dock.

We had to wait while one of the two ferry operators effected a repair to his bicycle which was leaning against the wall, and for which he had obviously just acquired spare parts on the town side of the dock, and then we were off. But not before one of the more adventurous children, dodging his parents eye for a moment, decided to ride his little bike, complete with stabilisers, at speed down the loading ramp to the sea!

He was deftly caught by the other ferry operator before he could launch himself from the end of the ramp into the sea a few feet below, admonished and handed back to his by now irritated parents, who confiscated the bicycle and were rewarded with floods of tears for their efforts.

The child soon calmed down as we got underway and the gentle swaying motion of the boat calmed frayed nerves.

For a few moments, as the tourists took photographs and little boats with fishing rods, larger boats with sundecks complete with sunbathers and a couple of wave-riders crossed our bows, the only sound, apart from the occasional sniff from the now bike-less child, was the gentle slap of the waves on the side of the boat and the subdued whirring of the electric motor.

As we looked around and drew level with the fishing fleet, now moored up and occupied only by hopeful seagulls, we were treated to views of the castle from a different angle. From the Town side of the bay it is only possible to glimpse parts of this magnificent ancient structure, up on it's hill, between the houses and shops crowded around the sea front area. But from here it was revealed in all its glory. It must have served it's original occupants well as a daunting threat to would be invaders and, although now softened with tumbling ivy and judicious planting and landscaping, it still makes a majestic statement to seafarers approaching the town.

The conversation on the ferry was getting up to speed again as we passed some of the opulent and luxurious boats moored, stern on, in this part of the bay. There was some pointing at one particular multi-storey vessel, this time moored side on, which at first glance was more ship than pleasure cruiser, and I picked up that this was the eighth largest super-yacht in the world and was visiting Denia to have some repairs. Presumably its mega-rich owners would be somewhere in the town mingling with the locals. Perhaps they would be sitting eating tapas with the owners of the other super-yachts at a table near us.

With his bicycle returned, the adventurous child tore off down the wide pavement where we docked and the gaggle of families followed at a more sedate pace. We saw them again a little later sitting outside a bar in the 'Glorietta' square; bikes and scooters neatly parked, and all on their best behaviour as they tucked into their lunch.

They occupied several tables pushed together, with the men, still discussing important matters, at one end and the women and children at the other.

By the looks of things, their Sunday ritual was being enjoyed by all.

Weekend rituals for some of the ex-pats in the more touristy areas are somewhat different, and perhaps not so pleasant.

One Sunday, as we travelled around the local towns and villages, we stopped for a drink in a place with the typical wide square filled with plastic chairs and tables, with broad umbrellas providing shade for the customers outside a crowded handful of bars.

We wondered what was going on when a waitress left the bar we were sitting near with a full bottle of Moet et Chandon champagne and went into one of the other bars, only to emerge a few moments later, still clutching the unopened bottle, and dash into a third.

It became obvious what was going on when we became aware of a group of people at an adjacent table, on which sat an ice bucket with an opened bottle in it; where the bull necked sweating man at its head was holding court.

As the waitress emerged from the third bar, this time triumphantly clutching a similar, but obviously cold bottle, we could not help overhearing the conversation.

'Abaht bladdy time too!' erupted bull neck, 'This one's empty!' and he inverted the bottle in the ice bucket to prove the point.

'As oi wass sayin' he droned to his less than rapt audience, who we suspected only hung around because he was obviously buying them drinks.

'As oi wass sayin, oi only drink Moet now. No beer,

no spirits ... well asept for the odd voddie. An' def-
nitlee no wine.'

He had obviously had quite enough of whatever
he was drinking and as the waitress approached
with the prized cold bottle, he added
'Wewl done, darlin', and get these muppets
wotevva they want too; An' one for you, sweet-
heart!'

The waitress backed away as soon as she was able
and deftly avoided a stout fingered hand which
was making a move towards patting her bottom.

'Nah where was oi? Oh yes ... I used to be best
friends wif a bloke called Jack Daniels, but that did
me 'ed in.' He chuckled at his own joke as he added,
'Oi fink moi second wife ran off wif 'im!'

He surveyed his audience to check they were lis-
tening and continued.
'Oi worked for ver biggest company in ver world.
In Russia and that. That's where oi discovered vis
stuff.' He tapped his glass appreciatively. 'Vis will
be moi third bottle today. Itsh all oi drink nah.'
He sniffed, settled a little more comfortably into
his chair and continued, 'Three bottles of Moet a
day an' vats moi limit. Cut it right dahn, Oi have!'

He made a lurch to raise himself from his seat
and, after a couple of staggers, found balance and
stepped over to stand by the bar next to the waitress, who backed away as his intentions became

obvious.

'Yoos really good, you are, getting me that cold one loik that! Oi've got five houses y'know! Oi could take you ta see vem, if you loik...'

We didn't wait to see any more and rescued the waitress by asking to pay our bill as we left.

We noticed, as we departed, that at least half of bull-neck's audience had also slipped away when he lurched to the bar, and those that remained were obviously checking their escape routes too.

For certain people the British Sunday lunch ritual in Spain is very different to the Spanish way of life; but, perhaps as long as we keep paying, our hosts do seem to tolerate our more uncouth moments. I wonder if the British would be so accommodating of visitors if the roles were reversed and this happened in England.

Bee asked me not to publish the tale of 'Bull-neck' because she felt it showed British ex-pats in a bad light and it was not at all typical of our experience in our chosen corner of Spain. It is true that 99% of the British ex-pats we have met have been absolutely charming, and that is why this incident stands out.

Generally, in our experience, those of our Countrymen who choose to settle in this part of Spain are delightful and we enjoy their company, especially when they integrate well with the Spanish.

This particular occasion was notable just because it was not typical and, gentle reader, I humbly ask you not to judge the British abroad on this one event.

DIVE!

All good things come to an end of course, and all too soon it was time for us to return to the U.K.

Amid all the razzmatazz, lies, intrigue, half truths, resignations and extravagant promises the Political world was immersed in, since Boris Johnson had declared a General Election would take place in early December, it was not going to be a peaceful homecoming.

As my own medical treatments could not be put off any longer, I was also in for a busy time.

My eldest son Richard, and his lovely partner Poppy had been to Mexico while we were away and were bubbling over with excitement. They couldn't wait to tell us all about their holiday; and Richard also had other news.

Ignoring the jet-lag, almost as soon as he got off the plane, Richard had his suit on and went for a meeting with the company who had headhunted him and offered him a new and exciting job just before they left for Cancun.

While Poppy slept it off, Richard was wrangling

himself a fine set of terms and conditions with his prospective new employer.

They invited us over to hear all their news when we got back, and Richard, with his redhead mother's pale skin but my dark hair was delighted to show us that, at last, he had managed to acquire a slight tan. He and his mother always had to slap on the factor 30, or 'ginger cream' as Richard called it, and he was always cross that, as he put it 'All you have to do is walk under a street lamp to get a tan, dad. It's just not fair!'
With an Afro-Caribbean father, Poppy had no such issues and had taken on an even more delightful shade of cinnamon in the Mexican sun and she teased Richard relentlessly about it.

I was only sorry that I had to burst the jolly bubble as I had some news for them too.

While David, my youngest son takes most things in his stride and is generally on an even keel, Richard, although clever and worldly wise, is more emotional, and I had not told him about my cancer diagnosis before we went away in case it spoilt his holiday. My boys are my whole life and I would do anything for them, and equally avoid doing anything that would upset them. Now however they had to be told, and I knew there would be tears.

Poppy had made one of her fabulous cheesecakes,

this time with salted caramel and popcorn, and fortunately that eventually lightened the mood. Although she told me Richard was very upset when we left, at least it was out in the open now. I had been dreading this moment.

As we left, with the rest of the cheesecake to bring home for David, things were back on a more steady emotional level, I think; but I hated having to put a damper on proceedings when they were obviously so excited to tell us what they had been up to.

We also told them about the drama on our flight back during which some poor soul had a fit or a heart attack five or six rows in front of us, and the plane had to make an emergency detour to land at Bordeaux where he could get medical attention.

When it was announced that we had to divert, we were also warned that we were going to have to land rapidly (presumably we had almost passed Bordeaux at full cruising height) and the pilot had to put the plane into a steep dive!

Now I know why they call it 'Queasy Jet'

Normally Bee and I experience an element of ear-popping and discomfort when coming in to land but there was none of that this time. I have never been on a modern jet airliner that performed a manoeuvre like this before and I confess it was a bit scary, but although we landed with something of a bump, it was reassuring to know that they can do these things if there is a medical emergency.

It added two hours to our flight while the paper-work was done and the plane was refuelled, and at least the poor guy was talking when they stretchered him off the plane, although we did not get any more updates on his condition.
When we landed in the UK a cold wind whipped into the plane as the door was opened and we knew we were home!

NO SAFARI NOW

On November 22nd 2019 I went for a bone scan at the local hospital.

I was lucky to get an appointment, and it was only the intervention of my Consultant that made it happen.

In January 2019, I found out, one of the three bone scanners at this hospital broke. In the summer of the same year the second one broke. There being no budget to repair or replace them, the hospital has soldiered on with just one scanner since and, needless to say, the department running it is very overstretched with the remaining scanner working almost continually.

The light on the horizon, i discovered, is that a 'business case' to replace the machines was prepared when the second unit broke down, but it was not approved until very recently and work on some alterations to the building and the installation of the replacement scanners will not commence until the budget to pay for them is available; in September 2020.

Meanwhile, I'm told, the hospital continues to lose nursing staff who are lured away by more lucrative positions in Europe and as far away as Australia, where they are offered more reasonable hours of work and much better terms and conditions and even, sometimes, there are promises of 'golden hello' payments to induce them to join. There are thousands of unfilled vacancies and the list grows almost daily. Across the country, as I write, there are 43,500 un-filled nurse vacancies.

As at December 2019, since the Referendum, 22,600 staff from the E.U. have left the NHS including at least 8,800 nurses and midwives.
Overall, at the point of the Referendum, 65,000 NHS staff were from the E.U., including 1 in 10 doctors; and between just January and October 2019, 3,252 staff from the E.U. left 50 hospitals, and that includes 1,116 nurses.
Now only 5% of the remaining nurses at Norfolk's flagship University hospital are from the E.U. and the number may well fall further. (Source: Eastern Daily Press and Independent newspaper Freedom of Information Requests December 2019).

That aside, as details of my own treatment have been decided and begin to be implemented. The lengthy timescales involved mean that I have had to let Bee down on a promise I made her when she retired, and cancel our safari 'trip of a lifetime' planned for June 2020.

Frankly this was a heartbreaking moment in my personal journey, at which the realities of having cancer really hit home and it all became much less surreal.

The suspicion that something was wrong first appeared early in 2019, and after a biopsy a few months later, the situation was confirmed. It took many months to get to that point and would take many more before I could finally meet a Consultant and start to move things forward.

If we had been living in Spain, matters would probably have been very different.

A week after my diagnosis was confirmed our good friend, the charming Holly Gunn, who lives in Spain, went to see her doctor.

Her visit, on a Tuesday, led to some tests and a biopsy being taken on the Thursday of the same week. By Monday she had her diagnosis and on the following Friday, after her consultant had checked the very latest position and best practice with the leading expert in the field in America, she started chemotherapy.

I was delighted for her that, in under a fortnight, she and the Spanish Health Service had moved her treatment forward. It had taken me just short of a year to achieve the same outcome in the UK, and at that point my treatment had still not started.

Perhaps we would have been wise to move to

Spain full time when we had the chance, but of course we didn't know this was going to happen then, and now the Brexit situation has made such a move impossible anyway.

As I wait for my next appointment letter, of course I wish Holly well, and I'm glad to report that as I went for my bone scan her first chemotherapy had been completed and she was taking a short holiday with her family in the UK.

In the meantime, my task will be to visit the travel agent to cancel our safari as it is likely to clash with a round of my own hospital based treatment.

The NHS do a wonderful job with the resources they have, but those resources are very limited and as a result Britain has slipped to the bottom of the Lancet's latest league table for cancer survival in high income countries. The report, published on 12/9/2019 'Lancet Oncology' points out that the difference between countries was partly explained by how quickly patients are diagnosed and get prompt access to effective treatments.

Hospitals in the UK are supposed to start cancer treatment within 62 days of GP referral in 85% of cases, but 94 out of 131 cancer services in England failed to reach that target during 2018/9.

Five years ago 36 out of 131 services missed this target, so things are getting worse.

Bee is philosophical however, and is sure that my

treatment will go to plan and we will be able to re-book our safari. There is hopefully a window in my diary in 2022.

A WALK AMONGST THE ORANGES AND AVOCADOS

All the waiting about gave me time to reflect on our discoveries in Spain.

At the entrance to our urbanisation there is a little rickety stall where Angel sells oranges and other produce grown on his adjacent smallholding.

He is not unique and, at the other end of the development, down one of the narrow country lanes beside the golf course, another smallholder offers her produce in a shady courtyard by her little house. She lays out the vegetables and fruits on a trestle table with an ancient weighing scale and smiles winningly at passers-by.

Between the two there is a patchwork of tiny landholdings, growing everything from aubergines to grapes with remarkable success, considering the notoriously poor soil.

These busy little farmers with their delightful two wheeled 'walking tractors', replacing the surprisingly recently retired donkeys, and inevitable rubber buckets are everywhere in this area and, against the odds on the steep rocky fields, they seem to be thriving.

Immediately adjacent to our apartment there are plantations of oranges and avocados, which although representing farming on a larger scale, are still really cottage industries, which are overseen by a small army of often elderly workers who produce quite remarkable quality and quantity from un-promising mountainside landholdings.

It is a delight to stroll around the lanes and tracks dividing these farmsteads and it is a reminder of the 'real Spain' on our doorstep.

Made possible by the slightly higher rainfall in this greenest part of the Costa Blanca, and aided by the still dependable centuries old Moorish irrigation system, it is quite remarkable what these farms are able to produce.

The landscape is peppered with little single room 'cortijos', which were originally used as stores and as somewhere to prepare a meal for the workers. These blocky, often ancient, and occasionally ornate structures do not always fulfil the rustic function they were built for, and one, along a little lane nearby, is quite clearly a retreat for a family and friends to enjoy themselves.
Painted bright blue, surrounded by plastic chairs, with paella pans hanging on the wall outside and set in an unkept field, with a newly concreted drive and parking for several cars; this little building is plainly more about enjoyment than toiling to produce crops.
With an empty beer barrel propping closed the substantial metal gate, a new plastic framed window in the front and a couple of wide promotional bar umbrellas leaning folded against one wall, even when unused during the working week it is clear to see that this does more than provide a crop store and respite from the sun for tired farmhands!

At the weekends, when tradition dictates that Spanish families return to their land, which is handed down through the generations, even if they wear suits and work in the cities during the week, perhaps this bright building represents how the younger generation intend to use their family smallholdings.

No doubt much more fun is had at this little cortijo than could be expected by those who still return to till the soil and tend the crops.

At least it is being used, unlike a plentiful collection of more derelict examples, which seem to be an abandoned, overgrown and half forgotten reminder of the rural tradition of generations of Spanish families, before the exodus to the towns to find paid work became all enveloping.

Several of these cortijos have been converted into dwellings, although the rules on living permanently on rural land are very strict. Whether legal or not, many have been extended and sit in carefully managed gardens, or are adorned with swings and slides for the youngsters and wide patio doors to enjoy the view.

Some are holiday homes and others seem to be occupied full time, but most seem to be well loved by the families that use them.

One or two have been 'enhanced' by their owners with balconies, a second storey, or ornate wrought ironwork; and several are hidden from prying eyes by vast solid metal sliding gates. Fair enough to protect a valuable vineyard or a productive orange grove, perhaps, but sometimes there is nothing at all behind these gates except

143

scrubby land and the remains of a rusting tractor or two.

We have seen noisy dogs, flocks of geese, donkeys, goats, sheep and even white peacocks in these little enclosures alongside all manner of tired and seemingly abandoned agricultural machinery. We were surprised to discover that one, just down the road, is used as a donkey sanctuary that serves 'gintonics' and beer to visiting supporters on a Sunday morning.

There is a vibrancy about these little communities which survives despite the inevitable population shift to work away, and it is fascinating to see the ingenious way these buildings and plots of land are 're-purposed' for the modern era.
Whether the Local Authority turns a blind eye or actually encourages these endeavours is not clear, but it all adds charm and colour to the 'campo' against a background of the fragrant orange blossom and the early morning bonfires of the farmers.

BARKING, BREXIT AND BORIS

I nevitably the renewal of Barkley's Pet Passport fell due at a time of uncertainty.

As I write it remains unclear whether Pet Passports will be recognised after Brexit and the cost of renewal, in terms of vaccinations required is, of course, not cheap.

Boris Johnson had called and won an election, having fought the nastiest campaign many can ever remember and, just before Christmas 2019, with a substantial majority, the new Government were able to remove some of the previously negotiated rights, concessions and benefits we might have enjoyed from their withdrawal agreement and ram it through Parliament. Now we really were leaving the EU but while it was not clear if Barkley's passport would be valid, it still had to be kept up to date.

Visiting the vet with Barkley is always a harrowing experience and not to be undertaken lightly.

Given that his defence mechanism when frightened is to employ his giant size bark, our tiny dog is not the most enchanting or encouraging prospect for any vet, and while ours did his best, it always took two members of staff to pin him down, and this time two visits to do what was necessary.

He was pleasant enough in the car, and although unsure in the waiting room, did not create a hullabaloo; but as soon as the vet put a stethoscope around his neck and asked Bee to lift him onto the examination bench, he was having none of it.

Being a rescue dog it is of course difficult to be sure what he went through in his early life. We knew he had been mistreated and was very easily frightened, but trips to the vet obviously triggered some unpleasant memory for him and, each time we had to go, the muzzle had to be deployed and it took two people to hold his wriggling little body and stop him bolting for the door. Unfortunately, on this occasion, he caught sight of the vet approaching with a syringe and with a yelp he lost control of his bladder and peed all down the vet's assistant's trousers!

After ten minutes of all-out warfare the vet conceded defeat and, on the basis that Barkley was becoming very stressed and could not be comforted, a further appointment was fixed to have another go in a few days time.

In the meantime Bee went to discuss the matter in our delightful local pet shop and purchase a more substantial muzzle, this time made of hard plastic rather than cloth, and in a fetching shade of National Health Hearing Aid Beige. She also bought some of his favourite treats to encourage a better attitude on the next visit.

The new muzzle worked, but the treats failed and the second bout was nearly as bad as the first. Although this time part of the necessary medication was delivered before the vet declared it was all becoming too much for him (I'm not sure if he meant the dog or the vet), and a halt to proceedings was called once again.

Fortunately, in terms of timing it had been possible to combine both Barkley's normal annual booster and the rabies jab required for the Pet Passport into one appointment. Unfortunately the part of the medicine still outstanding when the towel was thrown in on the second visit, was the rabies injection, so Barkley's Pet Passport could still not be renewed without yet another fight in the surgery.

Bee called a family meeting.

Because of Barkley's "issues" we had concerns about taking him abroad again and although, in a previous family council, we had convinced ourselves that he had calmed down a bit and we would give it another go, the situation was not ideal.

The dream of sitting outside some delightful beachside cafe and people watching over a drink and a tapa or two, with Barkley contentedly sitting at our feet under the table was just that; a dream. We knew we were unlikely to ever be able to pull it off, and it did mean that what we liked doing when in Spain and what Barkley found enjoyable were poles apart.

We tried it once and were told, following a formidable barking display, that we were welcome to visit the cafe in question but that, on reflection, the owner thought it would be rather better to leave Barkley at home next time. So that is what we did. Other than on his walks Barkley was mostly contented to stay in our air-conditioned apartment and sleep in a shaft of sunlight. But it wasn't fair on us, or on him, to allow this to become what we did when in our Spanish home.

Barkley, we decided, would be better off in England with our youngest son or in the friendly kennels where he had made great friends with the owners, when we went abroad.

None of us were very happy with this solution, although Barkley kept his thoughts to himself, but the decision had been made. Barkley's international reign of terror had come to an end.

But don't go thinking that we were not fond of Barkley; we love him and adore most of his funny little ways. It is just that bark that causes problems.

Indeed, when we first got him one of our neighbours even complained to the Council about his barking and for a while every time he went outside we dogged his every step, so to speak, and if he even so much as growled we snatched him up and bought him inside.

We have a good idea which neighbour it was but, being British, we have never raised the subject and let it pass. Suffice it to say that it was probably the owner of the house at the bottom of our garden, who regularly moves his wheelie bins about at odd times of day, and not always when the various collections we have are due.

The distinctive noise these bins make particularly annoys Barkley, and even when in the house he seems to pick up on it and gives voice.

The house in question is bristling with security cameras, one of which I am sure could see into our garden if these things have any sort of peripheral vision. Although it would be entirely unreasonable and fanciful to imagine that when their operator sees Barkley in the garden he goes and moves the bins deliberately to set him off!

A TAX DUE FOR *NOT* RENTING OUT OUR SPANISH HOLIDAY HOME?

The time of year had come around again when we had to tussle with the Spanish tax system and arrange to pay the most bizarre, and on the face of it unfair, tax you can imagine.

Non-residents who rent out their holiday homes have to submit regular returns and pax tax on their earnings. Fair enough you might say. But those, like us, who chose not to rent out our Spanish property still have to pay a tax ... on the earnings we *don't* make but *might* have collected if we had rented it out!

And, what is more, this barmy annual tax has to be calculated and paid separately on our garden store and on our garage as well as the apartment itself; and each has its own tax form!

To be fair, the amount involved is not much, and it's only once a year, but whoever heard of being taxed for not making any money!

In the first couple of years, when our solicitor told us this bonkers tax was due, we asked him to prepare the returns, known as Form 210, for us, and the fees being charged for this work were many times more than the tax itself.
We soon learned that there is a substantial cottage industry in the U.K. and in Spain of accountants and small enterprises offering to fill in the forms and get the tax paid for you at much more reasonable rates.

The tax itself has to be paid in person so, unless you know what you are doing and like queues, and happen to be in Spain when the forms need to be submitted, one also has to engage the services of that peculiar Spanish institution, the Gestor.

These individuals know their way around Spanish bureaucracy and can short circuit the often frustrating process of dealing with the tax authorities in all their guises; for a fee of course.

Happy the ex-pat who has found and tamed one of

these elusive characters, but of course we haven't, and we must rely on the little firms offering to fill in the forms (in Spanish of course) for another fee to get the job done. To be clear, though, these companies just fill in the forms and then pass them to their own favoured Gestor in Spain to submit them. Jobs for the boys then.

The tax itself only came to around €60, but the fees took the total cost to over £230, so it is not a cheap exercise and the truth of the matter is that I could not have completed the forms on my own. Doing it through the little agency we found was much cheaper than going through our solicitor, but it seems everybody involved still has to make a living, and of course the taxman will not be denied.

There is no point avoiding it however, because if you simply ignore this nutty tax and don't pay it, when you come to sell your property, assuming the authorities have not caught up with you in the meantime, the outstanding amounts, plus a fine will be deducted from the proceeds of your sale before you get the money!

A MENU WITH
NO CHOICES

My type of cancer comes with choices, I was told, which it is for the patient to make.

I was offered the opportunity to choose my preferred route on a photocopied information sheet I was handed.

The cancer charity I contacted beforehand was very helpful and offered me far more information, in the form of printed pamphlets about each procedure and the likely side effects; and their literature was much more comprehensive than the stuff the hospital gave me.

I was glad I didn't rely on the scant verbal or photocopied information I was initially given at the hospital as I now felt much better informed. However the hospital's own the literature did say that I would be given a blue folder at the 'Planning Meeting' with all the information I needed including diet sheets, advice on what to expect, what to wear, what to eat and drink and when, along with photographs of the machines they would use and the no doubt smiling staff I would encounter.

Having read the other pamphlets and explored the websites as directed, I now felt I understood the menu of options open to me and it was time to make my choice.

I elected to have the hormone therapy as a starter, followed by the radiotherapy; served over a seven and a half week period each workday with a rest at the weekends, as the main course.

I chose to drink only water, and to avoid caffeine and alcohol, and settled down to await events.

After an initial hiatus where the wrong variety of hormone therapy was prepared, but the mistake was noticed before it was served up, and with only a little delay, the choices for the main course now had to be made.

Having studied the details I decided I didn't fancy the operation route, although it could be served three ways. Robotic surgery sounded very space age and was perhaps the best of these options, followed by keyhole surgery or the more basic 'open surgery' involving a 20cm incision below the belly button and much delving about in the works to locate and remove the organ, but with no solid guarantee that the cancer would all be removed either.

The radiotherapy route also had choices, but only some suited me. Both types of brachytherapy were out because my cancer was too advanced and I needed something more substantial. External beam radiotherapy seemed to be the most commonly used solution, although there was proton beam therapy, stereotactic radiotherapy, conformal radiotherapy, intensity modulated radiotherapy, volumetric modulated arc therapy, image guided radiotherapy, 4D radiotherapy, radium 223 radioisotope therapy, and even the latest ultrasound and cryotherapy to be considered, and I read up about them all.

I was ready when a letter arrived with a date at the hospital for the long awaited 'Planning Meeting', which they promptly cancelled and then set it again for early January 2020.

I couldn't sleep the night before. This was it, things were going to happen at last.

Of course Bee and I arrived much to early and astonishingly found a parking space straight away, right outside the relevant hospital department's door. But what happened next was was very disappointing, not at all as promised and very depressing.

With little ceremony it was announced that my treatment could not now commence until March or April at the earliest because of staff shortages, no matter which of two treatments I now had to choose between.

I had thought this was supposed to be a 'planning clinic' which takes place just before your radiotherapy starts and includes a scan and a tattoo to permanently mark the spot to zap, but I was wrong.

The meeting was taken by a charming lady who very gently and considerately did her level best to convince me that I should consider having an operation rather than the radiotherapy and, I suspect, the real reason was that an operation is cheaper.

They have also cut back their radiotherapy offer, from a seven and a half week program of daily visits to give a 'fraction', as they call it, of the radiation dose in a controlled manner, giving the body time to recover after each session and at the weekends, to something quite different.
All they offer now is a four week course, where they deliver the same total dose of radiation but in much stronger larger 'fractions' and higher doses with only a minimum recovery period allowed. Needless to say this shortened course might mean less visits to the hospital but it is more risky and, when I probed a little deeper, they admitted it was more likely to have potentially unpleasant and life changing side effects.

Of course halving the time the course takes means the hospital can see twice as many patients; or the same number of patients with half the staff, depending on how you look at it. It emerged that staff shortages had also driven this policy change.

The operation they were encouraging me to consider instead removes the prostate entirely but not necessarily all the cancer, and there are three versions of this operation. The most modern and safest/least intrusive is the *'robotic'* surgery where the surgeon uses computer controlled devices, as I had found out. The next best is *'key hole'* surgery and the third, older and much more intrusive and potentially damaging is *'open surgery'* which is old tech and much more likely to be susceptible to infection and serious side effects.

Inevitably, it seemed to me, the only surgery option currently available at our local hospital is 'open surgery'.

However, I had decided that I would opt for radiotherapy and ask them to install a device called a *'Rectal Spacer'* beforehand to protect the rectum and bowel, which is particularly recommended where the quicker 'hotter' dose of radiation over a short course is used for people like me, with my history.

I had done a lot of research into this device and knew it was approved by the NHS and available to the hospital free of charge.

I was informed that while the device itself was free and very much recommended, the surgeon's time to install it was not going to be made available to me at this hospital.

If I liked, I could go to another hospital sixty miles away and have it installed (under general anaesthetic) privately at a cost yet to be finalised but likely to be between £10,000 and £20,000.

Or I could risk having the treatment without the Rectal Spacer.

I think the issue is that whilst the Spacer was approved by the NHS, it was not approved for funding (beyond an initial trial) by the politically controlled NICE which funds the NHS.

Further research has led me to believe that the reality of 'selling off the NHS' is much more nuanced than a simple sound bite. It seems to me (and this is only my opinion) that what is going on, and is likely to increase, is that devices such as the relatively new Rectal Spacer are going to be offered to patients (who soon enough we will probably be referring to as 'customers', no doubt) if the patient is prepared to pay.

This payment arrangement may inevitably become irresistible to NHS managers over time as budgets continue to be squeezed, and, I suspect, is likely to be be extended to drugs and then, heaven forbid, to Consultant's, doctors and nurses time in the future.

This is starting with new devices like the Rectal Spacer (which was developed by and is for sale through Boston Scientific, an American company) which the NHS will approve, and even recommended, but will not supply.

Possibly fine if you have and can afford private health insurance, which will obviously get progressively more expensive as this policy becomes the norm. But if no medical plan is available and you can't pay, you are left with only the option of the basic, though hopefully still effective treatments, offered at levels the budget will support by the supposedly 'free at the point of use' NHS.

I have no choice but to accept the increased risk of the hotter shorter high dose radiotherapy without the security of the Rectal Spacer, and it seems it is the only thing on the extensive menu that is really actually available.

I asked which of the three types of radiotherapy machines available to deliver this treatment they proposed to use. I should not have been surprised to learn that our hospital can currently only offer the more basic 'VMat' machine. They can't use the latest 'cutting edge' machines or any of the very latest tech, whether or not approved by the NHS and NICE (although routinely used abroad) ... because, I suspect, they might have the machines but, since the Brexit Referendum, given the exodus of EU nationals employed by the NHS, maybe they no longer have the trained staff to operate them!

Grim, isn't it. But before anybody gets on their high horse and all defensive, or takes any of this out of context, let me just say that all the staff I have met at our hospital and throughout the NHS have been wonderful, caring and keen to help. It is not their fault that the service has been held back and chronically underfunded; and they do their absolute best for their patients with the facilities that they do have. I am deeply grateful to them all and only sorry that they are not able to keep the NHS where it should be, and once was, at the leading edge of healthcare worldwide.

Our new Prime Minister, Boris Johnson, has made all sorts of promises about funding and developing the NHS and I only hope he delivers. The hard working, stressed out and overstretched staff in our amazing NHS certainly deserve more support and it is time they moved out of the funding waiting room and into the bright future the politicians keep promising.

Next up, for me, there was a discussion as to what would happen at the actual, yet to be re-arranged 'Planning Meeting' and subsequently on each consecutive day of treatment.

"We'll need to completely empty your bowels each time you come in."

What? Everyday?

"Yes, but it happens in private, so don't worry."

So colonic irrigation in a sparkling white tiled room, with stacks of neatly folded towels, scented candles and attendants in crisp white tunics, then?

"Well, no. We give you a box of suppositories and you put them in yourself in the loo."

There was a black line across each page of the indistinct photocopies I was handed at the end of the meeting. I remembered the original leaflet said I would be given a reassuring blue folder at this meeting with all the information I needed, complete with pictures.

It was not forthcoming.

Perhaps they ran out of those months ago. But my stapled photocopies have the handwritten website address at the top. All the information is probably on there and I could always print it off at home if I liked, I suppose.

Before we went into our somewhat depressing meeting, I had watched a procession of people using the water cooler by the reception desk.

It seemed to have run out or broken down judging by the conversation going on with the reception-ist, when one of the potential users complained. The stream of staff who kept using it to fill their water bottles were replaced by a solitary patient.

I felt for the thirsty patient.

He need not worry, though. There's a vending ma-chine with bottled water in the main reception and, if you don't have the right coins, there's a change machine near where you come in; by the ticket machine where you pay for your parking.

Oh, that's all right then. I expect we all have to pay for *something* along the way when we visit a hos-pital; although £10,000 plus for the simple spacer device was a bit of a shock.

What fun this was all turning out to be.

'Of course, if they can't start the treatment until March, we will miss the festival you wanted to go to in Spain' said Bee, just to add to my misery.

The literature I got from the charity said it could be helpful to set targets, and give yourself some-thing good to look forward to doing, when the treatment was finished.
I guess I would have to re-think that one and, as I digested this latest blow, it dawned on me that it was now exactly a year since the first symptoms cropped up.

Maybe next year then. If my luck holds.

SPAIN AGAIN?

But, I hear you ask, what about our adventures and discoveries in Spain?

After all, gentle reader, I would not like you to feel cheated if you bought this book to read more of our Spanish activities or to hear about the further antics of Barkley the dog, or other pets.

Obviously my cancer diagnosis and the ramifications of it has rather crowded my thoughts of late, and I hope you can forgive me. To compensate here is an anecdote from one of our recent visits, with stuff about Silke the cat in it...

Wine Merchant Graham has, we discovered, a penchant for old and classic cars, and quite a few exotic vehicles have passed through his hands over the years.

His current collection includes a wonderful 1955 Citroen 'Traction Avant', in quite twinkling condition; and a 2013 drop head Ford Mustang. Both have appeared in the adjacent garage area from time to time and, being a lover of old motors myself, have led to some interesting discussions.

Unlike some classic car owners, Graham does not hide the cars away or mollycoddle them, but uses them often and even drives the rumbling Mustang around Europe and to the UK, complete with Silke, the cat, perched on the passenger seat.

He admitted however that Silke is not so keen on the gorgeous old Citroen, which with it's limited and low range gearing is very noisy and struggles with the steep Spanish roads. But, although not her first choice, she still accompanies Graham on quite long trips into the mountains as he regularly stretches the antique Citroen's legs.

Until recently, the fearsome red Mustang has been annually pressed into service to transport Father Christmas or one (or perhaps all three) of the Three Kings around the nearby town in the appropriate season and, with the top down, it makes a commanding perch for the protagonists, sitting on the hood cover, to announce their arrival.

This year, however, the mighty Mustang is excused duties and is suffering with differential trouble.

Graham asked us if he could leave the car in our part of the garage for a few days, having collected it from its normal store, in preparation for the trip to a mechanic he had found nearby who professed to be able to fix it.

Fixing the problem had not been easy and this was to be the second try.

Clearly the parts for such a machine are unlikely to be available off the shelf in the typical Spanish garage, and the process of shipping them in, for the first go at a repair, took a little while. But once the parts were shipped from America and an attempt to fit them at a garage in Spain was unsuccessful, Graham had to start again with a different mechanic, and that is how it came to be sat, gleaming malevolently, in our garage while we were back in England dealing with other matters.

The first mechanic Graham decided to use spoke no English but had, always to hand, one of those gadgets which translate one language to another, which he used to communicate with his non-Spanish customers; of which, it seems, there were quite a few.

Thanks to this clever box of tricks Graham was able to establish that work could commence and the Mustang crunched and whined its way into the suitably untidy and oil be-grimed workshop.

When it emerged some time later, Graham took it for a spin and discovered that the car howled in protest with, on right hand turns, all sorts of noise from the drivetrain underneath.

Graham discussed his options
'It's a really crude car mechanically, but, not being common round here, it needs a mechanic that really knows what he is doing to sort it out.'

Presumably specialists in this type of car are rare on the Costa Blanca.

'But I do want to try to avoid having to have it put on a transporter and having it shipped, which is probably going to cost €2,000.'

Graham would know. He originally bought the car in Naples, Florida, and imported it into Spain, where it was registered.

He asked if he could park the car in our garage while he considered his options and, as we were back in England, we were happy to oblige.

That was the end of November, but now, as I write half way through January, the poorly car has still not been fixed.

Graham had discovered a British former racing car mechanic living in a tiny but very picturesque village high in the mountains a few miles inland. He obviously had experience of performance cars and said he could fix it, so Graham nursed the complaining Mustang up and down the steep and twisty roads to his door.

'Like the '65 one I had before, it hates corners, although with about 300 bhp on tap, going up the hills was no bother. But even though it's a 2013 model it's still a very crude car and being a fairly basic spec, is not what you'd call luxurious at the best of times'.

Compared to his sleek and powerful Mercedes Coupe 'everyday driver' it may not be sumptuously appointed, but it was clearly great fun in a snarly, no nonsense sort of way.

Being a sanguine character, and with the luxury of other transport to hand, Graham was philosophical. But as time went on he must have wondered what was taking so long.

I received regular updates in the form of slightly breathless text messages from Graham on such matters as confirmation that the latest 'Gota Fria' had caused no damage to the properties on the mountain, and on the battles he was having evicting an unruly tenant from another property he owned in the UK; but of the plight of the sickly Mustang there was no word.

On the 18th December however, he wrote:-

'Mustang is still at repairers and grumpy mechanic is quiet. This either means severe trouble and expense or nothing to worry about! I'm going to be optimistic on the basis that the car is basically so primitive. It might return for Christmas. We shall see!'

Needless to say there was no sign of it when on 27th December, Graham wrote:-

'Mustang still "on holiday". Work not started. Mechanic still stroppy.'

To a mechanic of his experience, Graham explained, this 'Diff issue' is no problem. But to finish the job, first he had to start!

However Graham's confidence was unshakable.
'He is a racing mechanic and a bit clever. So one puts up with his grumpiness!'

There was better news on 14th January. Graham's text read:-
'Mechanic is working on the Mustang! It was jacked up the other day, so we shall see, soon!'

I replied to the effect that I hoped it would be back soon and Graham enthused...
'Yes, it's great for driving to the U.K. and Silke likes it. She does not like traveling in the Citroen when I'm not using the Merc. I think she finds it too noisy!'

The intrepid and much travelled cat would have the last say on the choice of car for their next epic road trip across Europe, it seems!

GOING FOR A CHINESE

The plethora of Chinese run emporiums which crop up on just about every corner in most Spanish towns, selling an eclectic array of the essentials; from saucepans to solar lights, and the naff, from nylon blouses to plastic picture frames; are an institution not to be sneezed at.

If you want a peg or a patio chair, a mobile phone cover or a doormat, these stores will have it, and often in a choice of garish colours and unusual sizes.

They seem to be continually open too, and even in some places occupy premises next door to each other.

How they all survive I have no idea, particularly if you look at the prices they charge.

In the U.K. the nearest equivalent would perhaps be a cross between B&M (or Broken and Manky, as

I like to call it) and Poundland. But neither comparison really does these places justice.

They are unique, and I confess that I have often found a cheaper version there of whatever I set out to buy, five minutes after buying it in the 'normal' stores. I should learn my lesson.

You can even buy 'designer label' goods in these places; knock-offs of course, but sometimes with the designer names mis-spelt (although I suspect that the apparent spelling error on the knock-off versions of 'FC-UK' tee shirts might have been deliberate), and some of them are quite convincing.

Generally, if you are not too concerned about those designer labels and don't delve too deeply into the sustainable provenance of the materials used to produce everything from battery powered cuckoo clocks to beach hats, you can't go too wrong.

In the third store we tried, behind the wind up elastic band powered model aeroplanes and the inevitable golden plastic waving cats, we found what we were looking for.
Wine racks in various forms.

There were stackable plastic ones, splintery folding wooden ones, odd plastic coated wire ones in a choice of black or retina melting yellow, and even little cupboards with cut-outs for the bottles.

Our mission was to acquire racks for the multiplicity of bottles of wine Graham the Wine Merchant sold us.

We had the ideal place to put them; a small dark windowless utility room which remained cool in summer but, being in the centre of the building, was protected from the worst effects of any cold snap, which actually do occur sometimes, so I'm told!

We had the shelves to accommodate them too, but search as we might in the 'proper' shops, we had not been able to find wine racks until now.

In The U.K. I had a sort of wooden concertina affair and a metal and several rough timber things which held 24 bottles. Either sort would do but, in Spain we drew a blank until we finished up where perhaps we should have started, at the Chinese stores.

Initially we bought a very flimsy lightweight folding wooden one, but it folded when it should stand up and was not really up to the job. Smarting a little from the pinched finger this device dealt out, and lesson learned, on our second visit we chose stackable plastic ones. Two sets, enough for 24 bottles, and triumphantly adorned them with Graham's wines.

Our final choice works well, but must leak in some

way, because each time I go to look there never seem to be as many bottles on them as I expect!

I wish!

A MINOR VICTORY

On the 16th January I got some really good news for a change.

I had presented two sets of hospital consultants and oncologists with carefully highlighted copies of various NHS research documents and a plethora of press releases and case studies about the use of rectal spacers, and particularly the Boston Scientific "SpaceOAR" (organs at risk) device; and explained, pushed, begged and pleaded with them to consider my case and, somehow allow one of these devices to be installed before my 'radical radiotherapy' commenced - even if I had to pay for it myself.

Finally the consultants decided to call a meeting with experts, and the NHS management at the local hospital. Then, joy of joys, they phoned me to say that they accepted the position and would arrange to purchase and install twelve spacers (to be distributed on a first come first, served basis) to qualifying patients awaiting radiotherapy.

Needless to say I was first in the queue, and that position made clear, they decided to lock in my treatment, including the installation of the spacer at the local NHS hospital, and this time at the expense of the NHS!

The relief when I took the call was palpable.

The device was to be installed under general anaesthetic and, because it has a limited effective 'life' after installation, the dates of my radiotherapy, now due in March, would be fixed at last!

It might sound odd to say that getting them to agree to slash me open was a major success, but after what I had been through it really was.
And the icing on the cake was that the NHS were going to pay for it.

It felt good to know that eleven other patients would also benefit from this innovation and served to show that, if you really throughly do your homework, you can change minds; even when faced with the mighty and often immutable NHS.

I hope you never face a similar situation, gentle reader, but if you do, never give up.
Prepare your case with care and keep moving it up the chain of command until you get a sympathetic audience. And don't take 'No' for an answer!

LET'S HEAR IT
FOR BEE!

'Sorry, was I snoring again?'
"Yes. A bit. Why don't you go to bed."
The clock swam into view ... ten past nine.
It had happened again.

Since starting on hormone therapy I had experienced the common side effect of extreme tiredness, and along with the hot flushes, which inevitably woke me up, I was finding it hard to stay awake in the evenings, especially when I sat in my reclining chair in front of the TV.

Poor old Bee had a lot to put up with, and it was about to get worse. She would have to take me *every day* (except weekends) to the hospital, no doubt at some awkward hour, for four whole weeks, and sit about while I received my 'radical radiotherapy' treatment; but she never complains and always has a cheery disposition.

Although, as she put it, she 'didn't do sympathy', she did put up with a lot.

She finally said 'yes' and we got married in 1986, after meeting in the early eighties. But I knew she was the only girl in the world and I wanted to marry her as soon as I saw her.

She was working in the local pub not far from where we both lived at the time, in Surrey. It was a holiday job whilst she was completing her teaching degree in Canterbury.

I infested this particular pub with a blizzard of student nurses and a cast of ever changing staff from the local orthopedic hospital, whilst volunteering as a DJ on the hospital radio.
After the ward rounds, when we gathered requests, we invariably piled into my elderly battered short wheelbase Land Rover (without the roof when the sun shone) and clattered down the country lane to this pub for a refresher.

The record was ten, or was it eleven nurses and sundry hangers-on in the old seatbelt-less Land Rover. Not bad considering it had no seats at all in the back and bounced about all over the road. I'm fairly sure that nobody ever fell out either.

I confess that we didn't worry over much about

drinking and driving down the country lanes in those days and, no doubt after a pint or two, I announced to my fellow radio presenters and sundry medical personnel, pointing at Bee behind the bar (who fortunately had her back to us), that I was 'going to marry that girl' even though, at that stage I'm not sure I even knew her name.

I eventually plucked up courage to ask her out for a drink by asking her if she fancied a 'busman's holiday' visiting another pub with me, and she said "OK."

The beat up Land Rover was parked up and a more civilised car was used to take her to the delightful Scarlett Arms, in Walliswood, near Dorking.

Although very pretty, this ancient pub lacked some modern facilites in those days, and the antique landlady sat by an open carved wooden cash drawer on a bar stool, gazing into the middle distance.
She had to ease herself off the stool everytime someone ordered beer becuase the barrels, on stillages, sat in a back room and the beer had to be drawn off by hand from a tap in each one.

All the while she was away, the cash drawer remained open and, positioned as it was on the customer's side of the bar, it was quite vulnerable.
Nobody touched it, of course, but I doubt if the

clientele would be so trustworthy, or the staff so trusting, these days!

The Scarlett Arms worked enough of its magic to impress Bee though, and she consented to a second date.

By the time we got married, several years later, we had suffered a long distance relationship while she finished her degree and then worked in the East End of London.

In order to save some money she lived in a room in a filthy Victorian terrace with cockroaches and rampant damp for company. The house was due to be demolished and was let out by a shifty agent when it should not really have been occupied at all.

Her room was on the ground floor by the road and had a sliding sash window without a lock. It would be a simple matter to slide the sash up from the pavement outside and gain access.

My first action when she moved into this appalling place was to visit the ironmongers at the end of the road and buy a hammer and a six inch nail, which I knocked into the rotten frame and the surrounding timber to lock it solidly and permanently shut!

After that she moved to another shared house near Holloway jail and I took out a loan and bought a new car to cope with the travelling back and forth to see her.

Although she was very fond of it, her wheezing geriatric mini, with its black roof and red body-work, could not be relied upon; and it eventually could no longer even be trusted not to boil or lose the use of its brakes on the journey back to Surrey, so it had to go.

I insisted on driving her back after each weekend at home after that, as the area where she was living in London was hardly salubrious; and as a young girl on her own - and particularly *my* girl on her own, I took no risks with her safety.

And then I managed to get a decent job, put our finances on an even keel, convinced her to commute to work in a small but reputedly safe Volvo we had acquired, and we bought our first flat.

Nothing special, just one bedroom next door to the chip shop and on a busy road, but it was a start.

By the time we finally got married we were skint again, having sold the flat and bought a wreck of a 1930's house that had probably last been decorated in 1950, and needed everything doing. To help pay for all that, Bee made her own wedding dress and we held the reception in her mother's front room.

Things really took off after that and we moved a total of eleven times with my job. But Bee took it all in her stride, became an expert packer and uncomplainingly followed me about all over the country wherever my work led us next.

In 1990 we found ourselves living in a lovely tiny village with one streetlamp, one pub and a lot of fields. It had terrific views over The Somerset Levels, and was positioned on top of a hill quite close to the delightful town of Taunton. But things were looking difficult at work.

I had been shuttling between Cambridge and Taunton, spending two or three days in each location every week as the company I worked for struggled with the crash that the property market was going through. The travelling was horrendous, and exhausting, as you might imagine; and it couldn't go on.

Late one night, after the long drive back from Cambridge, where I had to stay in the same hotel in the middle of nowhere for two or three nights of each week, and could recite the unchanging menu blindfold after quite enough boring evenings there on my own, I had to deliver some news. 'Bee,' I said as I dragged myself through the front door, 'I've got some bad news. I think I'm going to be made redundant.'

"Thats a bugger," said Bee, "because I'm pregnant!"

We coped, of course. Our first son brightened our days and I soon got another job which moved us miraculously back to the same area of Surrey we had started off in; and a few years later our second son arrived, just before we had to move to Essex!

After that my hold on the corporate ladder became less tenuous and with just one more relocation, this time to rural Norfolk, we became a happy family all in one place.

So as you see, Bee has put up with a lot, and had to stifle any ambitions she may have had to trail about after me.

I was, and am, a very lucky man.

SO, WHAT NEXT?

Quite frankly I dont know.

It is the convention, in memoirs of this type to finish up with a 'tempter', perhaps in the form of the first chapter of the next book in the series, to encourage readers to buy the next one.

Of course I'd love to tell you about my ongoing adventures, and hopefully amuse you with more tales of my exploits, but the truth is I have no idea what the immediate or long term future holds for me now.

As I write, I am about to undergo surgery and then embark on treatments intended to cure my cancer and stop it spreading. I have been on hormone therapy for several months, which has had some unexpected side effects.

Although I'm told the results are reversible, I know that in the 1950's and 60's this treatment or something very like it was used to chemically castrate sex offenders and homosexuals, when that

sort of thing was illegal, and it was only later that its benefits in cancer treatment were discovered.
It was given to the likes of Alan Turing, inventer of the modern computer and cracker of the 'Enigma' machine. While his work shortened the war and changed our world forever as computers developed, these drugs also shortened his life and, unable to cope with the changes they inflicted on his mind as well as his body, he ultimately commited suicide.

I'm light years away from that, and the dose I'm on is probably just a tiny fraction of what he, and others like him had to endure, but some of the issues it throws up do create some concerns for me.

The idea is that the treatment stops, or at least slows down the growth of the cancer until it can be removed or destroyed by radiotherapy or chemotherapy, and the extreme fatigue and hot flushes which are the most obvious side effects are well worth enduring to achieve that.
But there are other things.

The bone scan indicated that it had not, so far, spread to my bones, and the uncomfortable lung investigation found no sign of it there; and more MRI and CT scans will check to see if it has progressed elsewhere. But, and this just might be an effect of the hormone therapy, I have found that my short term memory is becoming quite unreliable.

For example, I may perform some small task such as using and then putting the scissors back in the cupboard, and then moving on to another task; but I am disturbed by the thought that I cannot remember putting the scissors away, and I'll have to go and check. Sometimes more than once. Silly, and trivial I know, and possibly nothing to do with this at all, but a worry none-the-less.

In a more physical sense, the painkillers seem to last less and less time before I have to take more, and because I know they are quite strong and not to be messed with, I carefully write down what the clock says, each time I take them.
But I have to check the little pad where I record the times more and more often, and worry whether I remembered to write the time down last time I took them.

So, you see, I can't say what happens next; and until the treatment is complete, I don't think I'll be able to make any plans.
I want, more than anything, to return to Spain to stand once more on my terrace and admire the spectacular view from the mountain. And I want to continue to write about all the delightful people, places and adventures we have there, but when, or even whether that will happen is now

not in my control.

I hope to write for you again one day, and, if you can bear to read any more, please do keep an eye out for a new sequel. I've even thought up a snappy and original title for it and I think I'll call it 'Even More Spain Tomorrow'.
But for that tomorrow to come, first we have to get through today.

◆ ◆ ◆

If you enjoyed this book I would be really grateful if you left an Amazon review, even if it is just one sentence. Thank you.

Check out all my books at:-
https://www.goodreads.com/book/show/50716257-more-spain-tomorrow

INFORMATION

Contacts:

You can email me at **bobable693@gmail.com**

You can also follow/friend me on **Facebook** by searcing for **'Bob Able'** or register for updates on my website:-

https://bobable693.wixsite.com/spaintomor-row

A percentage of the net proceeds of
this book will be presented to
'The Big C', Norfolk's Cancer Charity.

For more details visit
big-c.co.uk/support

Please note:
This memoir reflects the author's recollections of experiences over a period of time. In order to preserve the anonymity of the people he writes about, some names and locations have been changed. Certain individuals are composites, and dialogue and events have been created from memory, and in some cases, compressed to facilitate a natural narrative.

Copyright Bob Able 2020

First Edition

The author reserves all rights. No part of this publication (ebook or printed versions) may be used in any manner whatsoever without written permission except in the case of brief quotations embodied in critical articles or reviews.
The author asserts the moral right under the Copyright, Design and Patents Act 1988 to be identified as the author of this work.
All rights reserved. No part of this publication (ebook or printed versions) may be reproduced, stored in a retrieval system, transmitted, in any form or by any means without the prior written consent of the author, nor be circulated in any form of cover other than that in which it is pub-

lished and without a similar condition being imposed on the subsequent purchaser.

PRAISE FOR AUTHOR

Praise for 'Spain Tomorrow'.

Very entertaining and well written.

Wonderful read!

Like chatting to an old friend.

I loved this book!

I enjoyed this light read very much.

A great book.

Very funny and interesting.

Nicely written.

BOOKS IN THIS SERIES

Spain Tomorrow

When Bob and his long suffering wife, Bee, un-expectedly inherit almost enough money to buy a holiday home in Spain, everything looks rosy. But this was the middle of the Brexit Referendum chaos; when the UK Government imploded, exchange rates fell through the floor, and nobody seemed to know what the future held. Was this a sensible time to be buying property in Spain? Probably not, but Bob and Bee ploughed on anyway!

Read how they discovered the delights of the less touristy bits of the Costa Blanca and met a host of charming characters, while almost everything in the apartment broke and nobody seemed to know who owned the road!

Printed in Great Britain
by Amazon

51346675R00121